A History of Western Civilization

THE EMERGENCE OF MODERN EUROPE

c. 1500 TO 1788

A History of Western Civilization

THE EMERGENCE OF MODERN EUROPE

c. 1500 TO 1788

EDITED BY HEATHER M. CAMPBELL, SENIOR EDITOR,
GEOGRAPHY AND HISTORY

IN ASSOCIATION WITH

Published in 2011 by Britannica Educational Publishing
(a trademark of Encyclopædia Britannica, Inc.)
in association with Rosen Educational Services, LLC
29 East 21st Street, New York, NY 10010.

Distributed exclusively by Rosen Educational Services.
For a listing of additional Britannica Educational Publishing titles, call toll free (800) 237-9932.

First Edition

Britannica Educational Publishing
Michael I. Levy: Executive Editor
J.E. Luebering: Senior Manager
Marilyn L. Barton: Senior Coordinator, Production Control
Steven Bosco: Director, Editorial Technologies
Lisa S. Braucher: Senior Producer and Data Editor
Yvette Charboneau: Senior Copy Editor
Kathy Nakamura: Manager, Media Acquisition
Heather M. Campbell: Senior Editor, Geography and History

Rosen Educational Services
Alexandra Hanson-Harding: Editor
Nelson Sá: Art Director
Cindy Reiman: Photography Manager
Matthew Cauli: Designer, Cover Design
Introduction by Charles Doersch

Library of Congress Cataloging-in-Publication Data

The Emergence of Modern Europe : c. 1500 to 1788 / edited by: Heather M. Campbell. — 1st ed.
    p. cm. — (A history of western civilization)
In association with Britannica Educational Publishing, Rosen Educational Services.
Includes bibliographical references and index.
ISBN 978-1-61530-343-4 (library binding)
    1. Europe—Civilization—16th century. 2. Europe—Civilization—17th century. 3 Europe—
Civilization—18th century. 4. Civilization, Modern. 5. History, Modern. I. Campbell,
Heather M.
CB401.E44 2011
940.2'32—dc22

                                                                        2010014511

Manufactured in the United States of America

On the cover: This painting by Pieter Snayers shows the Battle of Thionville (Diedenhofen)
in 1639. It was one of the many fierce battles of the Thirty Years' War, which raged across
Europe from 1618 to 1648. *Imagno/Hulton Archive/Getty Images*

On page viii: *Winter Landscape #3*, painted by Pieter Bruegel, the Younger (1564–1638),
shows everyday life in the Netherlands. *SuperStock/Getty Images*

On pages 1, 32, 58, 92, 152, 188, 231, 234, 236: Maria Theresa at age 35. The archduchess of
Austria and queen of Hungary and Bohemia (1740–80) and empress of the Holy Roman Empire,
she was one of the most influential leaders of her time. *Imagno/Hulton Archive/Getty Images*

CONTENTS

Modern Europe—the geographical, political, economic, and cultural entity we recognize today—began to take shape between 1500 and 1788. The traditional view of the Renaissance, the European intellectual and cultural revival of the 1400s and 1500s, was that Europe had experienced a rebirth of reason following the thousand years of ignorance known as the "Dark Ages." Of course, history is never that simple, and the Middle Ages, the period stretching roughly between the 5th and 15th centuries, was not truly a time of incredible ignorance and cultural backwardness. Still, if we were to travel back in time to the Europe of the Middle Ages, we would find its locally based political and socioeconomic structures largely strange to us. If we jumped ahead to the 1500s, however, we would find the "reborn" Europe increasingly recognizable in its national political organization, its expanding economies and cities, and its growing understanding of itself. This was the start of early modern Europe.

If the 1500s were an exciting time of prosperity and discovery, they were also a period of disillusionment, when Europe lost forever the unity of its religious belief. If the 1600s saw a thrilling explosion of scientific discovery, philosophic inquiry, and the emergence of modern European values, they also witnessed horrific eruptions of religious wars that killed millions, bankrupted kingdoms, and left towns and farms in smoking ruins. While the 1700s raised up the banner of the Enlightenment, which preached the power of the human mind to liberate and improve people's lives, that banner fell at the end of the century in a paroxysm of revolution, continent-wide war, and rabid nationalism that tore Europe apart. But as this volume will show, through the clouds of conflict and reaction from 1500 to 1788, the European trend toward greater economies, a greater consideration of the role of the state, greater tolerance, and greater individual freedom became increasingly clear.

Early modern Europe's economy and society grew more firmly capitalist during the 1500s. Trade and commerce flourished. New markets opened up, and the Continent found itself part of a world economic system. Capital now not only affected how economies organized themselves but also increasingly influenced politics and international relations.

This was a heady time for many people. After two centuries of decline, recession, plague, famine, and war, things were finally looking up. Overall, Europe in 1500 had only a fraction of the population it had had two centuries earlier. Since more work was available now than there were workers, wages increased. Fewer people meant less demand, so the prices of land, livestock, food, goods, and services fell. Cheap food meant people could afford a better diet. Falling prices also meant this was a good time to invest in new enterprises with better technology. As the population began to increase, towns grew, cities grew, and the middle class grew. With them grew banks, financial institutions, and money markets—and these became more integrated.

This kind of growth was facilitated by the early modern state, which was centralized, with an organized bureaucracy and army, and with its authority vested in a strong executive, usually a monarch. An orderly state could provide fertile ground for business and finance. Indeed, the centralized state was also a consumer, purchasing goods for its own support, as well as weapons for its military; it was also a client of banks, taking out loans and investing.

But ironically enough, all this prosperity and economic development did not take place in a context of peace and mutual understanding. It took place in the context of religious division and war. Martin Luther's criticism of some of the practices of the Roman Catholic Church, his call for reform, and the papacy's violent reaction ignited a socio-political and confessional firestorm that permanently changed the cultural mentality of Europe. Religiously uni-fied Europe was fractured into a hostile hodgepodge of Protestant states and Catholic states.

While the Protestant Reformation and Catholic Counter-Reformation unequivocally divided Europe, Europeans still yearned for religious uniformity. Although it may seem odd to us now, persecuted religious minorities in early modern Europe did not favour tolerance or free-dom of worship. Europeans believed there was only one true religion—their own. All other beliefs were danger-ously false, even evil. Thus, conformity was the only moral solution to religious differences. Using force to return people to religious truth might save their eternal lives. Moreover, unlike the empires of Islam, which allowed Muslims, Christians, and Jews to worship relatively freely, Christian Europe generally viewed diversity as a threat. Conformity, Europeans felt, meant social cohesion and prosperity.

The result of this mentality was, perhaps not surpris-ingly, religious war. The first round broke out in the Holy Roman Empire in the mid-1500s but did not last long, as no one had the military advantage. Lutheran and Catholic rulers then signed the Peace of Augsburg in 1555, whereby the necessary evil of toleration was formally instituted—but only among the various states of the empire. No toleration was expected within each state, where the offi-cial religion was determined by the religion of the ruler. Everyone believed that a country could have only *un roi*, *une loi*, *une foi*: one king, one law, one faith.

Soon enough, other religious wars erupted. In France, brutal civil war carried on for three dozen years. Meanwhile the Netherlands and Spain fought an on-again, off-again religious war for more than 80 years. And so the yearning for order grew, especially in the Holy Roman Empire with its jigsaw puzzle of about a thousand semiautonomous political units, where any question of dynastic succession could change the balance of power between Protestants and Catholics, and where the Habsburg emperor was a fervent Roman Catholic. As far as he was concerned, the heretical Protestants within his empire constituted a source of chronic instability. They could appeal to foreign powers for aid or influence against their emperor, and in an age when European rulers were consolidating their power through increased conformity, this was intolerable.

At the same time, other rulers in Europe—even fellow Catholics—were deeply troubled by how powerful the Habsburg dynasty had become. The tradition since the Renaissance had been for states to ally whenever necessary to maintain a balance of power, so that no state or dynasty could triumph over the rest. But now the Habsburgs had grown into a worldwide superpower: they ruled the Holy Roman Empire, Spain, much of the Netherlands, and portions of Italy; they also controlled Spain's vast holdings in the Americas.

When the Holy Roman emperor tried to impose Catholicism on Bohemia, Protestant nobles rebelled, thus sparking the Thirty Years' War (1618–48), a more destructive conflict than ever had been seen in Europe—one that would decimate the German heartland and kill millions. At first, it was clearly a religious war, with Protestant forces outmatched by Catholic armies, which were backed by Spanish Habsburg wealth and the power of the papacy. Then, however, more states were drawn into the conflict, as they saw opportunities for political gain and a chance to weaken the mighty Habsburgs. Soon the war was being fought less for religious reasons than for political ones. Finally, with the Peace of Westphalia in 1648, the war ended in exhaustion and desolation.

The results of the war were several: the Netherlands had gained independence from Habsburg Spain; the latter had been replaced by France as the great power of Europe; the member states of the Holy Roman Empire won complete sovereignty; and the emperor found himself left with little more than a symbolic role. More important, from this point on, the balance of power doctrine prevailed, foreign policy became increasingly secular, and the essential structure of modern Europe as a community of sovereign states was established. Yet from all this fragmentation, paradoxically, a growing European identity was emerging: philosophers, scientists, and artists had begun addressing a larger European audience, not just compatriots.

Nevertheless, the attitude of the 1600s could be described as one of pessimism. In fact, doubt seemed to be the spirit of the age. After all, even as scientists discovered that what Europeans had traditionally believed about the nature of life and the world was quite wrong, so too philosophers now called into question the very nature of knowledge, of what could be known, and of what constituted truth. This, clearly, had implications for the reliability and authority of church teaching and religious belief. Meanwhile, daily life for people became increasingly difficult as the economy fell into recession and agricultural production became strained by the limits of cultivation technology. Even the century's weather grew steadily colder.

During this time of insecurity, early modern European nation-states saw their rulers take on increasing authority to ensure the good order of the state, and many thinkers of the time agreed that this was needed. Absolutism, already prevalent in the 1500s, became the political institution of the 1600s, growing more absolute. Rulers now claimed God's authority in ruling both secular and religious institutions. But in order for monarchs to consolidate authority, they had to suppress any internal competition, such as the privileges of the nobles. After all, aristocrats had certain rights, which a monarch could not legally violate. These rights in turn protected or affected those peasants who lived on the lands of the nobles. Hence, a monarch often felt that noble privileges entangled him or her in a web of interlocking and competing obligations and restrictions, weakening the power and prosperity of the state. The most successful absolute monarchs of this time, such as Louis XIV of France, succeeded in neutralizing competing allegiances. Nevertheless, the Netherlands and England, both prosperous and powerful, were two outstanding examples that absolute monarchy was not necessary for success.

As the 1600s came to their close, Europe, already spreading its power and influence worldwide through colonization and trade, experienced an accumulating confidence in itself—in the superiority of its developments in science, technology, navigation, and exploration, as well as in its recognition of the power of reason to liberate and improve. This optimistic attitude, part of a tradition stretching back to the humanism of the Renaissance, was now reinforced and given impetus by the Scientific Revolution's insistence on the rational and the empirical, and on a vigorous humanistic critique of society and culture by the philosophes.

The philosophes were various thinkers, primarily in 18th-century France, who were so remarkably prolific in their writing and publishing that all of Europe buzzed with the ideas they proposed. They rejected the superstitious and divisive aspects of religious belief as barbaric remnants from the ignorant past, and they argued for toleration of different religious beliefs, education, social responsibility, an end to torture, an end to slavery, freedom of speech, and more. The 1700s became known as the *siècle des Lumières*—"age of the Enlightened ones." *Lumière*, or "light," was also the metaphor for "reason" itself, which the philosophes believed was the best means for clearly understanding the world and improving the human condition. The philosophes saw themselves as cosmopolitans—as citizens of Europe—and they popularized many 17th- and 18th-century discoveries to open Europeans' eyes to this newfound knowledge.

Were they in agreement on all issues? No. Did their arguments change social practices or government policies? Sometimes. Were the philosophes at times contradictory? Yes. For example, although many Enlightenment thinkers argued that absolutism was the ideal government, as long as the monarchs themselves were enlightened, some most assuredly did not. Eventually, the views of those who believed in democratic institutions, governmental checks and balances, and the constitutional guarantees of liberty and individual rights became more persuasive. In fact, it was during the late 18th century that British colonies in North America rose up in revolution and established a democratic republic based on Enlightenment principles. By century's end another revolution—in France, the heart of the Enlightenment—had overthrown one of the longest-standing monarchies in history in the name of *liberté, égalité, fraternité* ("liberty, equality, brotherhood"). Although the "light" of the Enlightenment would be eclipsed for a time by extremism, war, and destructive nationalism, many of the philosophes' values would win out in the coming centuries.

Early modern Europe developed into a community of nation-states sharing scientific knowledge, technological developments, and, perhaps most important, values and ideas. This community of nations worked together to keep any one from politically or militarily dominating the rest. It developed a worldwide economy with financial systems and money markets, production mechanisms, and commercial distribution networks. It had a growing and increasingly prosperous middle class, while questions of liberty, equality under the law, and the responsibility of government became embedded in the international conversation. Here we see a Europe more and more familiar to our understanding, the modern Europe we recognize.

European Economy and Society, c. 1500–1648

The 16th century was a period of vigorous economic expansion. This expansion in turn played a major role in the many other transformations—social, political, and cultural—of the early modern age. By 1500 the population in most areas of Europe was increasing after two centuries of decline or stagnation. The bonds of commerce within Europe tightened, and the "wheels of commerce" (in the phrase of the 20th-century French historian Fernand Braudel) spun ever faster. The great geographic discoveries then in process were integrating Europe into a world economic system. New commodities, many of them imported from recently discovered lands, enriched material life. Not only trade but also the production of goods increased as a result of new ways of organizing production. Merchants, entrepreneurs, and bankers accumulated and manipulated capital in unprecedented volume. Most historians locate in the 16th century the beginning, or at least the maturing, of Western capitalism. Capital assumed a major role not only in economic organization but also in political life and international relations. Culturally, new values—many of them associated with the Renaissance and Reformation—diffused through Europe and changed the ways in which people acted and the perspectives by which they viewed themselves and the world.

This world of early capitalism, however, can hardly be regarded as stable or uniformly prosperous. Financial crashes were common; the Spanish crown, the heaviest borrower in Europe, suffered repeated bankruptcies (in 1557, 1575–77, 1596, 1607, 1627, and 1647). The poor and destitute in society became, if not more numerous, at least more visible. Even as capitalism advanced in the West, the once-free peasants of central and eastern Europe slipped into serfdom. The apparent prosperity of the 16th century gave way in the middle and late periods of the 17th century to a "general crisis" in many European regions. Politically, the new centralized states insisted on new levels of cultural conformity on the part of their subjects. Several states expelled Jews, and almost all of them refused to tolerate religious dissenters. Culturally, in spite of the revival of ancient learning and the reform of the churches, a hysterical fear of witches grasped large segments of the population, including the learned. Understandably, historians have had difficulty defining the exact place of this complex century in the course of European development.

THE ECONOMIC BACKGROUND

The century's economic expansion owed much to powerful changes that were already under way by 1500. At that time, Europe comprised only between one-third and one-half the population it had possessed about 1300. The infamous Black Death of 1347–50 principally accounts for the huge losses, but plagues were recurrent, famines frequent, wars incessant, and social tensions high as the Middle Ages ended. The late medieval disasters radically transformed the structures of European society—the ways by which it produced food and goods, distributed income, organized its society and state, and looked at the world.

The huge human losses altered the old balances among the classical "factors of production"—labour, land, and capital. The fall in population forced up wages in the towns and depressed rents in the countryside, as the fewer

2

workers remaining could command a higher "scarcity value." In contrast, the costs of land and capital fell; both grew relatively more abundant and cheaper as human numbers shrank. Expensive labour and cheap land and capital encouraged "factor substitution," the replacement of the costly factor (labour) by the cheaper ones (land and capital). This substitution of land and capital for labour can be seen, for example, in the widespread conversions of arable land to pastures; a few shepherds, supplied with capital (sheep) and extensive pastures, could generate a higher return than plowland, intensively farmed by many well-paid labourers.

Capital could also support the technology required to develop new tools, enabling labourers to work more productively. The late Middle Ages was accordingly a period of significant technological advances linked with high capital investment in labour-saving devices. The development of printing by movable metal type substituted an expensive machine, the press, for many human copyists. Gunpowder and firearms gave smaller armies greater fighting power. Changes in shipbuilding and in the development of navigational aids allowed bigger ships to sail with smaller crews over longer distances. By 1500 Europe achieved what it had never possessed before: a technological edge over all other civilizations. Europe was thus equipped for worldwide expansion.

Social changes also were pervasive. With a falling population, the cost of basic foodstuffs (notably wheat) declined. With cheaper food, people in both countryside and city could use their higher earnings to diversify and improve their diets—to consume more meat, dairy products, and beverages. They also could afford more manufactured products from the towns, to the benefit of the urban economies. The 14th century is rightly regarded as the golden age of working people.

Economic historians have traditionally envisioned the falling costs of the basic foodstuffs (cereals) and the continuing firm price of manufactures as two blades of a pair of open scissors. These price scissors diverted income from countryside to town. The late medieval price movements thus favoured urban artisans over peasants and merchants over landlords. Towns achieved a new weight in society; the number of towns counting more than 10,000 inhabitants increased from 125 in about 1300 to 154 in 1500, even as the total population was dropping. These changes undermined the leadership of the landholding nobility and enhanced the power and influence of the great merchants and bankers of the cities. The 16th would be a "bourgeois century."

Culturally, the disasters of the late Middle Ages had the effect of altering attitudes and in particular of undermining the medieval faith that speculative reason could master the secrets of the universe. In an age of ferocious and unpredictable epidemics, the accidental and the unexpected, chance or fate, rather than immutable laws, seemed to dominate the course of human affairs. In an uncertain world, the surest, safest philosophical stance was empiricism. In formal philosophy, this new priority given to the concrete and the observable over and against the abstract and the speculative was known as nominalism. In social life, there was evident a novel emphasis on close observation, on the need to study each changing situation to arrive at a basis for action.

The 16th century thus owed much to trends originating in the late Middle Ages. It would, however, be wrong to view its history simply as a playing out of earlier movements. New developments proper to the century also shaped its achievements. Those developments affected population; money and prices; agriculture, trade, manufacturing, and banking; social and political institutions;

and cultural attitudes. Historians differ widely in the manner in which they structure and relate these various developments; they argue over what should be regarded as causes and what as effects. But they are reasonably agreed concerning the general nature of these trends.

DEMOGRAPHICS

For the Continent as a whole, the population growth under way by 1500 continued over the "long" 16th century until the second or third decade of the 17th century. A recent estimate by the American historian Jan De Vries set Europe's population (excluding Russia and the Ottoman Empire) at 61.6 million in 1500, 70.2 million in 1550, and 78.0 million in 1600; it then lapsed back to 74.6 million in 1650. The distribution of population across the Continent was also shifting. Northwestern Europe (especially the Low Countries and the British Isles) witnessed the most vigorous expansion; England's population more than doubled between 1500, when it stood at an estimated 2.6 million, and 1650, when it probably attained 5.6 million. Northwestern Europe also largely escaped the demographic downturn of the mid-17th century, which was especially pronounced in Germany, Italy, and Spain. In Germany, the Thirty Years' War (1618–48) may have cost the country, according to different estimates, between 25 and 40 percent of its population.

Cities also grew, though slowly at first. The proportion of Europeans living in cities with 10,000 or more residents increased from 5.6 percent of the total population in 1500 to only 6.3 percent in 1550. The towns of England continued to suffer a kind of depression, now often called "urban decay," in the first half of the century. The process of urbanization then accelerated, placing 7.6 percent of the population in cities by 1600, and even continued during the 17th-century crisis. The proportion of population in cities of more than 10,000 inhabitants reached 8.3 percent in 1650.

More remarkable than the slow growth in the number of urban residents was the formation of cities of a size never achieved in the medieval period. These large cities were of two principal types. Capitals and administrative centres—such as Naples, Rome, Madrid, Paris, Vienna, and Moscow—give testimony to the new powers of the state and its ability to mobilize society's resources in support of courts and bureaucracies. Naples, one of Europe's largest cities in 1550, was also one of its poorest. The demographic historian J.C. Russell theorized that Naples' swollen size was indicative of the community's "loss of control" over its numbers. Already in the 16th century, Naples was a prototype of the big, slum-ridden, semiparasitic cities to be found in many poorer regions of the world in the late 20th and early 21st centuries.

Commercial ports, which might also have been capitals, formed a second set of large cities: examples include Venice, Livorno, Sevilla (Seville), Lisbon, Antwerp, Amsterdam, London, Bremen, and Hamburg. About 1550, Antwerp was the chief port of the north. In 1510, the Portuguese moved their trading station from Brugge to Antwerp, making it the chief northern market for the spices they were importing from India. The Antwerp bourse, or exchange, simultaneously became the leading money market of the north. At its heyday in mid-century, the city counted 90,000 inhabitants. The revolt of the Low Countries against Spanish rule (from 1568) ruined Antwerp's prosperity. Amsterdam, which replaced it as the greatest northern port, grew from 30,000 in 1550 to 65,000 in 1600 and 175,000 in 1650. The mid-17th century—a period of recession in many European regions—was Holland's golden age. Late in

Life wasn't all hardship in early modern Europe. This 1650 painting by artist Jan Steen shows a lively scene in a Dutch tavern. Hulton Archive/ Getty Images

the century, Amsterdam faced the growing challenge of another northern port, which was also the capital of a powerful national state—London. With 400,000 residents by 1650 and growing rapidly, London then ranked below only Paris (440,000) as Europe's largest city. Urban concentrations of such magnitude were unprecedented; in the Middle Ages, the largest size attained was roughly 220,000, reached by a single city, Paris, about 1328.

Another novelty of the 16th century was the appearance of urban systems, or hierarchies of cities linked together by their political or commercial functions. Most European cities had been founded in medieval or even in ancient times, but they long remained intensely competitive, duplicated each other's functions, and never coalesced during the Middle Ages into tight urban systems. The more intensive, more far-flung commerce of the early modern age required a clearer distribution of functions and cooperation as much as competition. The centralization of governments in the 16th century also demanded clearly defined lines of authority and firm divisions of functions between national and regional capitals.

TRADE AND THE "ATLANTIC REVOLUTION"

The new importance of northwestern Europe in terms of overall population and concentration of large cities reflects in part the "Atlantic revolution," the redirection of trade routes brought about by the great geographic discoveries. The Atlantic revolution, however, did not so much replace the old lines of medieval commerce as build upon them. In the Middle Ages, Italian ports—Venice and Genoa in particular—dominated trade with the Middle East and supplied Europe with Eastern wares and spices. In the north, German cities, organized into a loose federation known as the Hanseatic League, similarly dominated Baltic trade. When the Portuguese in 1498 opened direct maritime links with India, Venice faced the competition of the Atlantic ports, first Lisbon and Antwerp. Nonetheless, Venice effectively responded to the new competition and attained in the 16th century its apogee of commercial importance; in most of its surviving monuments, this beautiful city still reflects its 16th-century prosperity. Genoa was not well placed to take advantage of the Atlantic discoveries, but Genoese bankers played a central role in the finances of Spain's overseas empire and in its military ventures in Europe. Italians did not quickly relinquish the prominence as merchants and bankers that had distinguished them in the Middle Ages.

In the north, the Hanseatic towns faced intensified competition from the Dutch, who from about 1580 introduced a new ship design (the *fluitschip*, a sturdy, cheaply built cargo vessel) and new techniques of shipbuilding, including wind-powered saws. Freight charges dropped and the size of the Dutch merchant marine soared; by the mid-17th century, it probably exceeded in number of vessels all the other mercantile fleets of Europe combined. The English competed for a share in the Baltic trade, though they long remained well behind the Dutch.

In absolute terms, Baltic trade was booming. In 1497 the ships passing through the sound separating Denmark from Sweden numbered 795; 100 years later the number registered by the toll collectors reached 6,673. The percentage represented by Hanseatic ships rose over the same century from roughly 20 to 23–25 percent; the Germans were not yet routed from these eastern waters.

In terms of maritime trade, the Atlantic revolution may well have stimulated rather than injured the older exchanges. At the same time, new competition from the western ports left both Hanseatics and Italians vulnerable to the economic downturn of the 17th century. For both the Hanseatic and Italian cities, the 17th—and not the 16th—century was the age of decline. At Lübeck in 1628, at the last meeting of the Hanseatic towns, only 11 cities were represented, and later attempts to call a general meeting ended in failure.

PRICES AND INFLATION

In historical accounts, the glamour of the overseas discoveries tends to overshadow the intensification of exchanges within the Continent. Intensified exchanges led to the formation of large integrated markets for at least some commodities. Differences in the price of wheat in the various European regions leveled out as the century progressed, and prices everywhere tended to fluctuate in the same direction. The similar price movements over large areas mark the emergence of a single integrated market in cereals. Certain regions came to specialize in wheat production and to sell their harvests to distant consumers. In particular, the lands of the Vistula basin, southern Poland, and Ruthenia (western Ukraine) became regular suppliers of grain to Flanders, Holland, western Germany, and, in years of poor harvests, even England and Spain. In times of famine, Italian states also imported cereals from the far-off Baltic breadbasket. From about 1520, Hungary emerged as a principal supplier of livestock to Austria, southern Germany, and northern Italy.

Changes in price levels in the 16th century profoundly affected every economic sector, but in ways that are disputed. The period witnessed a general inflation, known traditionally as the "price revolution." It was rooted in part in frequent monetary debasements; the French kings, for example, debased or altered their chief coinage, the *livre tournois*, in 1519, 1532, 1549, 1561, 1571–75 (four mutations), and 1577. Probably more significant (though even this is questioned) was the infusion of new stocks of precious metal, especially silver, into the money supply. The medieval economy had suffered from a chronic shortage of precious metals. From the late 15th century, however, silver output, especially from German mines, increased and remained high through the 1530s. New techniques of sinking and draining shafts, extracting ore, and refining silver made mining a booming industry. From 1550 "American treasure," chiefly from the great silver mine at Potosí in Peru (now in Bolivia), arrived in huge volumes in Spain, and from Spain it flowed to the many European regions where Spain had significant military or political engagements. Experts estimate (albeit on shaky grounds) that the stock of monetized silver increased by three or three and a half times during the 16th century.

At the same time, the growing numbers of people who had to be fed, clothed, and housed assured that coins would circulate rapidly. In monetary theory, the level of prices varies directly with the volume of money and the velocity of its circulation. New sources of silver and new numbers of people thus launched (or at least reinforced) pervasive inflation. According to one calculation, prices rose during the century in nominal terms by a factor of six and in real terms by a factor of three. The rate is low by modern standards, but it struck a society accustomed to stability. As early as 1568 the French political theorist Jean Bodin perceptively attributed the inflation to the growing volume of circulating coin, but many others, especially those victimized by inflation, chose to blame it on the greed of monopolists. Inflation contributed no small part to the period's social tensions.

Inflation always redistributes wealth; it penalizes creditors and those who live on fixed rents or revenues; it rewards debtors and entrepreneurs who can take immediate advantage of rising prices. Moreover, prices tend to rise faster than wages. For the employer, costs (chiefly wages) lag behind receipts (set by prices), and this forms what is classically known as "profit inflation." This profit inflation has attracted the interest of economists as well as historians; especially notable among the former is the great British economic theorist John Maynard Keynes. In a treatise on money published in 1930, he attributed to the 16th-century price revolution and profit inflation a crucial role in the primitive accumulation of capital and in the birth of capitalism itself. His analysis has attracted much criticism. Wages lagged not so much behind the prices of manufactured goods as of agricultural commodities, and inflation may not have increased profits at all. Then, too, inflation in Spain (particularly pronounced in the 1520s), or later in France, did not lead to a burst of enterprise. There is no mechanical connection between price structures and behaviour.

On the other hand, the price revolution certainly stimulated the economy. It clearly penalized the inactive. Those who wished to do no more than maintain their traditional standard of living had, nonetheless, to assume an active economic stance. The increased supply of money seems further to have lowered interest rates—another advantage for the entrepreneur. The price revolution by itself did not assure capital accumulation and the birth of capitalism, but it did bring about increased outlays of entrepreneurial energy.

LANDLORDS AND PEASANTS

The growing population in the 16th century and the larger concentrations of urban dwellers required abundant supplies of food. In the course of the century, wheat prices steadily rose; the blades of late medieval price scissors once more converged. Money again flowed into the countryside to pay for food, especially wheat. But the social repercussions of the rising price of wheat varied in the different European regions.

In eastern Germany (with the exception of electoral Saxony), Poland, Bohemia, Hungary, Lithuania, and even eventually Russia, the crucial change was the formation of a new type of great property, called traditionally in the German literature the *Gutsherrschaft* (ownership of an estate). The estate was divided into two principal parts: the landlord's demesne, from which he took all the harvest; and the farms of the peasants, who supplied the labour needed to work the demesne. The peasants (and their children after them) were legally serfs, bound to the soil. These bipartite, serf-run estates superficially resemble the Classical manors of the early Middle Ages but differ from them in that the new estates were producing primarily for commercial markets. The binding of the peasants of eastern Europe to the soil and the imposition of heavy labour services constitute, in another traditional term, the "second serfdom."

In the contemporary west (and in the east before the 16th century), the characteristic form of great property was the *Grundherrschaft* ("ownership of land"). This was an aggregation of rent-paying properties. The lord might also be a cultivator, but he worked his land through hired labourers.

What explains the formation of the *Gutsherrschaft* in early modern eastern Europe? Historians distinguish two phases in its appearance. The nobility and gentry, even without planning to do so, accumulated large tracts of abandoned land during the late medieval population collapse. However, depopulation also meant that landlords could not easily find the labour to work their extensive holdings. Population, as previously mentioned, was growing again by 1500, and prices (especially the price of cereals) steadily advanced. Inflation threatened the standard of living of the landlords; to counter its effects, they needed to raise their incomes. They accordingly sought to win larger harvests from their lands, but the lingering shortage of labourers was a major obstacle. As competition for their labour remained high, peasants were prone to move from one estate to another, in search of better terms. Moreover, the landlords had little capital to hire salaried hands and, in the largely rural east, there were few sources of capital. They had, however, one recourse. They dominated the weak governments of the region, and even a comparatively strong ruler, like the Russian tsar, wished to accommodate the demands of the gentry. In 1497 the Polish gentry won the right to export their grain without paying duty. Further legislation bound the peasants to the soil and obligated them to work the lord's demesne. The second serfdom gradually spread over eastern Europe; it was established in Poland as early as 1520; in Russia it was legally imposed in the Ulozhenie (Law Code) of 1649. At least in Poland, the western market for cereals was a principal factor in reviving serfdom, in bringing back a seemingly primitive form of labour organization.

No second serfdom developed in western Europe, even though the stimulus of high wheat prices was equally powerful. Harassed landlords, pressed to raise their revenues, had more options than their eastern counterparts. They might look to a profession or even a trade or, more commonly, seek at court an appointment paying a salary or a pension. The western princes did not want local magnates to dominate their communities, as this would erode their own authority. They consequently defended the peasants against the encroachments of the gentry. Finally, landlords in the west could readily find capital. They could use the money either to hire workers or to improve their leased properties, in expectation of gaining higher rents. The availability of capital in the west and its scarcity in the east were probably the chief reasons why the agrarian institutions of eastern and western Europe diverged so dramatically in the 16th century.

In the west, in areas of plow agriculture, the small property remained the most common productive unit. However, the terms under which it was held and worked differed widely from one European region to another. In the Middle Ages, peasants were typically subject to a great variety of charges laid upon both their persons and the land. They had to pay special marriage and inheritance taxes; they were further required to provide tithes to the parish churches. These charges were often small—sometimes only recognitive—and were fixed by custom. They are often regarded as "feudal" as distinct from "capitalist" rents, in that they were customary and not negotiated; the lord, moreover, provided nothing—no help or capital improvements—in return for the payments.

The 16th century witnessed a conversion—widespread though never complete—from systems of feudal to capitalist rents. The late medieval population collapse increased the mobility of the peasant population; a peasant who settled for one year and one day in a "free village" or town received perpetual immunity from personal charges. Personal dues thus eroded rapidly; dues weighing upon the land persisted longer but could not be raised. It was therefore in the landlord's interest to convert feudal tenures into leaseholds, and this required capital.

In England upon the former manors, farmers (the original meaning of the term was "leaseholder" or "rent payer"), who held land under long-term leases, gradually replaced copyholders, or tenants subject only to feudal dues. These farmers constituted the free English yeomanry, and their appearance marks the demise of the last vestiges of medieval serfdom. In the Low Countries, urban investors bought up the valuable lands near towns and converted them into leaseholds, which were leased for high rents over long terms. The heavy infusions of urban capital into Low Country agriculture helped make it technically the most advanced in Europe, a model for improving landlords elsewhere. In central and southern France and in central Italy, urban investment in the land was closely linked to a special type of sharecropping lease, called the *métayage* in France and the *mezzadria* in Italy. The landlord (typically a wealthy townsman) purchased plots, consolidated them into a farm, built a house upon it, and rented it. Often, he also provided the implements needed to work the land, livestock, and fertilizer. The tenant gave as rent half of the harvest. The spread of this type of sharecropping in the vicinity of towns had begun in the late Middle Ages and was carried vigorously forward in the 16th century. Nonetheless, the older forms of feudal tenure, and even some personal charges, also persisted, especially in Europe's remote and poorer regions. The early modern countryside presents an infinitely complex mixture of old and new ways of holding and working the land.

Two further changes in the countryside are worth noting. In adopting Protestantism, the North German states, Holland, the Scandinavian countries, and England confiscated and sold, in whole or in part, ecclesiastical properties. Sweden, for example, did so in 1526–27, England in 1534–36. It is difficult to assess the exact economic repercussions of these secularizations, but the placing of numerous properties upon the land market almost surely encouraged the infusion of capital into (and the spread of capitalist forms of agrarian organization in) the countryside.

Second, the high price of wheat did not everywhere make cereal cultivation the most remunerative use of the land. The price of wool continued to be buoyant, and this, linked with the availability of cheap wheat from the east, sustained the conversion of plowland into pastures that also had begun in the late Middle Ages. In England this movement is called "enclosure." In the typical medieval village, peasants held the cultivated soil in unfenced strips, and they also enjoyed the right of grazing a set number of animals upon the village commons. Enclosure meant both the consolidating of the strips into fenced fields and the division of the commons among the individual villagers. As poorer villagers often received plots too small to work, they often had little choice but to sell their share to their richer neighbours and leave the village. In 16th-century England, enclosure almost always meant the conversion of plowland and commons into fenced meadows or pastures. To many outspoken observers, clergy and humanists in particular, enclosures were destroying villages, uprooting the rural population, and multiplying beggars on the road and paupers in the towns. Sheep were devouring the people—"Where there have been many householders and inhabitants," the English bishop Hugh Latimer lamented, "there is now but a shepherd and his dog." In light of recent research, these 16th-century enclosures were far less extensive than such strictures imply. Nonetheless, enclosures are an example of the power of capital to transform the rhythms of everyday life; at the least, they were an omen of things to come.

In Spain, sheep and people also entered into destructive competition. Since the 13th century, sheepherding had fallen under the control of a guild known as the Mesta; the guild was in turn dominated by a few grandees. The Mesta practiced transhumance (alternation of winter and spring pastures); the flocks themselves moved seasonally along great trailways called *cañadas*. The government, which collected a tax on exported wool, was anxious to raise output and favoured the Mesta with many privileges. Cultivators along the *cañadas* were forbidden to fence their fields, lest the barriers impede the migrating sheep. Moreover, the government imposed ceiling prices on wheat in 1539. Damage from the flocks and the low price of wheat eventually crippled cereal cultivation, provoked widespread desertion of the countryside and overall population decline, and was a significant factor in Spain's 17th-century decline. High cereal prices primarily benefited not the peasants but the landlords. The landlords in turn spent their increased revenues on the amenities and luxuries supplied by towns. In spite of high food costs, town economies fared well.

PROTOINDUSTRIALIZATION

Historians favour the term "protoindustrialization" to describe the form of industrial organization that emerged in the 16th century. The word was initially applied to cottage industries in the countryside. In spite of the opposition of urban guilds, rural residents were performing many industrial tasks. Agricultural labour did not occupy the peasants during the entire year, and they devoted their free hours to such activities as spinning wool or weaving and washing cloth. Peasants usually worked for lower remuneration than urban artisans. Protoindustrialization gave rural residents supplementary income, which conferred a certain immunity from harvest failures; it enabled them to marry younger and rear larger families; it prepared them, socially and psychologically, for eventual industrialization. The efforts of urban guilds to limit rural work enjoyed only limited success; in England, for example, the restrictions seem rarely to have been enforced. Cottage industries certainly existed in the Middle Ages, but the economic expansion of the 16th century diffused them over much larger areas of the European countryside, perhaps most visibly in England and western Germany.

More recently, historians have stressed the role of towns in this early form of industrial organization. Towns remained the centres from which the raw materials were distributed in the countryside. Moreover, urban entrepreneurs coordinated the efforts of the rural workers and marketed their finished products. Certain processes—usually the most highly skilled and the most remunerative—remained centred in cities. Not only the extension of industry into rural areas but also the greater integration of city and countryside in regional economies was the principal achievement of 16th-century industry.

This manner of organizing manufacturers is known as the "putting-out system," an awkward translation of the German *Verlagssystem*. The key to its operation was the entrepreneur, who purchased the raw materials, distributed them among the working families, passed the semifinished products from one artisan to another, and marketed the finished products. He was typically a great merchant resident in the town. As trade routes grew longer, the small artisan was placed at ever-greater distances from sources of supply and from markets. Typically, the small artisan would not have the knowledge of distant markets or of the preferences of distant purchasers and rarely had the money to purchase needed raw materials. The size of the trading networks and the volume of merchandise moving within them made the services of the entrepreneur indispensable and subordinated the workers to his authority.

The production of fabric remained everywhere the chief European industry, but two developments, both of them continuations of medieval changes, are noteworthy. In southern Europe the making of silk cloth, stimulated by the luxurious tastes of the age, gained unprecedented

prominence. Lucca, Bologna, and Venice in Italy and
Sevilla and Granada in Spain gained flourishing industries.
Even more spectacular in its rise as a centre of silk manufacture was the city and region of Lyon in central France.
Lyon was also a principal fair town, where goods of northern and southern Europe were exchanged. It was ideally
placed to obtain silk cocoons or thread from the south and
to market the finished cloth to northern purchasers. The
silk industry is also notable in that most of the workers it
employed were women.

Northern industry continued to concentrate on woolens but partially turned its efforts to producing a new
type of cloth, worsteds. Unlike woolens, worsteds were
woven from yarn spun from long-haired wool; moreover,
the cloth is not fulled (that is, washed, mixed with fuller's
earth, and pounded in order to mat the weave). Worsteds
were lighter and cheaper to make than woolens and did
not require the services of a mill, which might have to be
located near running water. Under the name of "new drap-
eries," worsteds had come to dominate the Flemish wool
industry in the late Middle Ages. In the 16th century, several factors—the growth of population and of markets, the
revolt of the Low Countries against Spain, and religious
persecutions, which led many skilled Protestant workers
to seek refuge among their co-religionists—stimulated
the worsted industry in England. England had developed
a vigorous woolens industry in the late Middle Ages, and
the spread of worsted manufacture made it a European
leader in fabric production.

Another major innovation in 16th-century industrial
history was the growing use of coal as fuel. England, with
rich coal mines located close to the sea, could take particular advantage of this cheap mineral fuel. The port of
Newcastle in Northumbria emerged in the 16th century as
a principal supplier of coal to London consumers. As yet,

coal could not be used for the direct smelting of iron, but it found wide application in glassmaking, brick baking, brewing, and the heating of homes. The use of coal eased the demand on England's rapidly diminishing forests and contributed to the growth of a coal technology that would make a crucial contribution to the later Industrial Revolution.

In industry, the 16th century was not so much an age of dramatic technological departures; rather, it witnessed the steady improvement of older technological traditions — in shipbuilding, mining and metallurgy, glassmaking, silk production, clock and instrument making, firearms, and others. Europe slowly widened its technological edge over non-European civilizations. Most economic historians further believe that protoindustrialization, and the commerce that supplied and sustained it, best explains the early accumulations of capital and the birth of a capitalist economy.

GROWTH OF BANKING AND FINANCE

Perhaps the most spectacular changes in the 16th-century economy were in the fields of international banking and finance. To be sure, medieval bankers such as the Florentine Bardi and Peruzzi in the 14th century and the Medici in the 15th had operated on an international scale, but the full development of an international money market with supporting institutions awaited the 16th century. Its earliest architects were South German banking houses, from Augsburg and Nürnberg in particular, who were well situated to serve as financial intermediaries between such southern capitals as Rome (or commercial centres such as Venice) and the northern financial centre at Antwerp. Through letters of exchange drawn on the various bourses that were growing throughout Europe, these bankers were able to mobilize capital in fabulous amounts. In 1519 Jakob II Fugger the Rich of Augsburg amassed nearly two million florins for the Habsburg king of Spain, Charles I, who used the money to bribe the imperial electors (he was successfully elected Holy Roman emperor as Charles V). Money was shaping the politics of Europe.

The subsequent bankruptcies of the Spanish crown injured the German bankers; from 1580 or even earlier, the Genoese became the chief financiers of the Spanish government and empire. Through the central fair at Lyon and through letters of exchange and a complex variant known as the *asiento*, the Genoese transferred great sums from Spain to the Low Countries to pay the soldiers of the Spanish armies. In the mid-16th century, dissatisfied with Lyon, the Genoese set up a fictional fair, known as Bisenzone (Besançon), as a centre of their fiscal operations. Changing sites several times, Bisenzone from 1579 settled at Piacenza in Italy.

POLITICAL AND CULTURAL INFLUENCES ON THE ECONOMY

The centralized state of the early modern age exerted a decisive influence on the development of financial institutions and in other economic sectors as well. To maintain its power both within its borders and within the international system, the state supported a large royal or princely court, a bureaucracy, and an army. It was the major purchaser of weapons and war matériel. Its authority affected class balances. Over the century's course, the prince expanded his authority to make appointments and grant pensions. His control of resources softened the divisions among classes and facilitated social mobility. Several great merchants and bankers, the Fuggers among them, eventually were ennobled. Yet, in spending huge sums on war, the early modern state may also have injured the economy. The floating debt of the French crown came close to 10 million ecus (the ecu was worth slightly less than a gold florin), that of the Spanish, 20 million. These sums probably equaled the worth of the circulating coin in the two kingdoms. Only in England did the public debt remain at relatively modest proportions, about 200,000 gold ducats. Governments, with the exception of the English, were absorbing a huge part of the national wealth. The Spanish bankruptcies were also sure proof that Spain had insufficient resources to realize its ambitious imperial goals.

The effort to control the economy in the interest of enhancing state power is the essence of the political philosophy known as mercantilism. Many of the policies of 16th-century states affecting trade, manufactures, or money can be regarded as mercantilistic, but as yet they did not represent a coherent economic theory. The true age of mercantilism postdates 1650.

Cultural changes also worked to legitimate, even to inspire, the early modern spirit of enterprise. In a famous thesis, the German sociologist Max Weber and, later, the English historian Richard Henry Tawney posited a direct link between the Protestant ethic, specifically in its Calvinist form, and the capitalist motivation. Medieval ethics had supposedly condemned the profit motive, and teachings about usury and the just price had shackled the growth of capitalist practices. Calvinism made the successful merchant God's elect. Today, this thesis appears too simple. Many movements contributed to a reassessment of the mercantile or business life, and the rival religious confessions influenced one another. Calvinism did not really view commercial success as a sign of God's favour until the 17th century, but 16th-century Roman Catholic scholastics (as the humanists before them) had come to regard the operations of the marketplace as natural; it was good for the merchant to participate in them. Martin Luther, in emphasizing that every Christian had received a calling (*Berufung*) from God, gave new dignity to all secular employments. Roman Catholics developed their own theory of the "vocation" to both secular and religious callings in what was a close imitation of the Lutheran *Berufung*.

ASPECTS OF EARLY MODERN SOCIETY

To examine the psychology of merchants is to stay within a narrow social elite. Historians, in what is sometimes called "the new social history," have paid close attention to the common people of Europe and to hitherto neglected social groups—women, the nonconformists, and minorities.

Two fundamental changes affected the status of early modern women. Women under protoindustrialization were valued domestic workers, but they also had little economic independence; the male head of the household, the father or husband, gained the chief fruits of their labour. A second change, perhaps related to the first, was the advancing age of first marriage for women. Medieval girls were very young at first marriage, barely past puberty; these young girls were given to mature grooms who were in their middle or late 20s. By the late 16th century, parish marriage registers show that brides were nearly the same age as their grooms and both were mature persons, usually in their middle 20s. This is, in effect, what demographers call the modern, western European marriage pattern. Comparatively late ages at first marriage also indicate that significant numbers of both men and women would not marry at all. Though the origins of this pattern remain obscure, it may be that families, recognizing the economic value of daughters, were anxious to retain their services as long as possible. European marriages were overwhelmingly patrilocal — that is, the bride almost always joined her husband's household. Thus, the contribution that daughters made to the household economy exerted an upward pressure on their ages of marriage. Whatever the explanation for the new marriage pattern, the near equality of ages between the marriage partners at least opened the possibility that the two would become true friends as well as spouses; this was harder to achieve when brides were young girls and their husbands mature and experienced.

In investigating what might be called the cultural underground of the early modern age, historians now take full advantage of a distinctive type of source. The established religions of Europe, both Roman Catholic and Protestant, zealously sought to assure uniformity of belief in the regions they dominated. The courts inspired by them actively pursued not only the heterodox but also witches, the insane, and anyone who maintained an unusual style of life. The special papal court known as the Inquisition operated in many (though not all) Catholic states. Its judges carefully interrogated witnesses and kept good records. These records permit rare views into the depths of early modern society. They show how widespread was the belief in magic and the practice of witchcraft and how far popular culture diverged from the officially sanctioned ideologies. The variety and strange nature of popular beliefs have convinced some historians that Christianity had never really won the minds of rural people during the Middle Ages. Only the aggressive and reformed churches of the 16th century succeeded in converting the peasants to formal Christianity. This thesis may be doubted, but it cannot

King James VI of Scotland (later James I of England) examines women accused of being witches in 1591. English School/The Bridgeman Art Library/Getty Images

be doubted that the European countryside sheltered deep wells of popular culture which the documentation of the age leaves largely in darkness.

Witchcraft presents special problems. Witches were hunted in the 16th century with a relentlessness never seen before. Were they becoming more numerous, their

Malleus Maleficarum

The *Malleus Maleficarum* ("The Hammer of Witches") was a detailed legal and theological document (c. 1486) regarded as the standard handbook on witchcraft, including its detection and its extirpation, until well into the 18th century. Its appearance did much to spur on and sustain some two centuries of witch-hunting hysteria in Europe. The *Malleus* was the work of two Dominicans: Johann Sprenger, dean of the University of Cologne in Germany, and Heinrich (Institoris) Kraemer, professor of theology at the University of Salzburg, Austria, and inquisitor in the Tirol region of Austria. In 1484 Pope Innocent VIII issued the bull *Summis Desiderantes*, in which he deplored the spread of witchcraft in Germany and authorized Sprenger and Kraemer to extirpate it.

The *Malleus* codified the folklore and beliefs of the Alpine peasants and was dedicated to the implementation of Exodus 22:18: "You shall not permit a sorceress to live." The work is divided into three parts. In Part I the reality and the depravity of witches is emphasized, and any disbelief in demonology is condemned as heresy. Because of the nature of the enemy, any witness, no matter what his credentials, may testify against an accused. Part II is a compendium of fabulous stories about the activities of witches — e.g., diabolic compacts, sexual relations with devils (incubi and succubi), transvection (night-riding), and metamorphosis. Part III is a discussion of the legal procedures to be followed in witch trials. Torture is sanctioned as a means of securing confessions. Lay and secular authorities are called upon to assist the inquisitors in the task of exterminating those whom Satan has enlisted in his cause.

The *Malleus* went through 28 editions between 1486 and 1600 and was accepted by Roman Catholics and Protestants alike as an authoritative source of information concerning satanism and as a guide to Christian defense.

services more in demand? It may be that the two reformations, Protestant and Catholic, purged Europe of the magical aura that the medieval church had hung over it. It may be that the abiding thirst for enchantment could be slaked only in the cultural underground, only

Section of Venice, Italy, that in the early modern era was a Jewish ghetto. Photograph. Imagno/Hulton Archive/Getty Images

through popular magic. But it may also be that the new determination and efficiency of the reformed religions and the early modern states simply exposed persons long a fixture in village life: the woman healer, who knew the ancient, time-honoured cures; the old wife, who through charms or potions could induce conception or sterility, love or hate. It is hard even to reconstruct the character of early modern witchcraft. Terrorized witnesses tended to respond in ways they thought would please their interrogators; thus they reinforced stereotypes rather than revealing what they truly believed or did. Court records of this kind are not flawless sources, but they remain a rich vein of cultural history. Ironically, the court officials saved for history the thoughts and values they had hoped to extirpate.

The 16th century also witnessed a continuing deterioration in the status of western Jews. They had been expelled from England in 1290 and from France in 1306 (the first of several expulsions and readmissions). Riots and killings accompanying the Black Death (the Jews were accused of poisoning the wells) had pushed the centres of German Jewry (the Ashkenazim) to the east, into Poland, Lithuania, and, eventually, the Russian Empire. In 1492 the Jews of Spain (the Sephardim), who had formed the largest and most culturally accomplished western community, were given the choice of conversion or expulsion. Many chose to leave for Portugal (whence they would also be subsequently expelled), the Low Countries, Italy, or the Ottoman Empire. Those who remained and ostensibly converted were called "New Christians," or Marranos, and many of these later chose to emigrate to more hospitable lands. Many Marranos continued to live as Jews while professing Christianity; accusations against them were commonly heard by the

Inquisition in both Spain and Italy. Their position was especially distressing. Often, both Jews and Christians rejected them, the former for their ostensible conversion, the latter for secretly practicing Judaism.

The communities of exiles had different experiences. Jews in Holland made a major contribution to the country's great prosperity. The Italian states, papal Rome included, accepted the exiles, hoping to profit from their commercial and financial expertise. Yet the Jews were also subject to increasingly severe restrictions. The Jewish community at Venice, which absorbed large numbers of Iberian Jews and Marranos, formed the first ghetto (the word itself is Venetian, first used in 1516). The practice of confining Jews into walled quarters, locked at night, became the common social practice of early modern states, at least in the central and eastern parts of the Continent. The Sephardim, who continued to speak a form of Spanish known as Ladino, established large and prosperous colonies in Ottoman cities — Salonika, Istanbul, and Cairo among them. On balance, however, the early modern period in Europe was socially and culturally a dark age for Jewry.

Is there a single factor that can explain the social history of Europe's 16th century? Many have been proposed: population growth, overseas discoveries, the emergence of a world economic system, American treasure, profit inflation, capital accumulation, protoindustrialization, the Renaissance or Reformation. Perhaps the most decisive change was progress toward more integrated systems of social organization and action and toward wider and tighter social networks. The western monarchies overcame much of the political localism of the medieval world and set a model that even divided Italy and Germany would eventually emulate.

Economic integration advanced even more rapidly; markets in foodstuffs, spices, luxuries, and money extended throughout the Continent: The skilled banker could marshal funds from all the Continent's money markets; silks from Lucca were sold in Poland. Cities formed into hierarchies, still on a regional basis but surpassing in their effectiveness the loose associations of medieval urban places. To be sure, competition among the centralized states often led to destructive wars and terrible waste of resources; and the quest for unity brought shameful persecution upon those who could not or would not conform to the dominant culture.

CHAPTER 2

EUROPEAN POLITICS AND DIPLOMACY, C. 1500–1648

The 16th and early 17th centuries constituted a new political era in Europe. By the close of the 15th century, changes in the structure of European polity, accompanied by a new intellectual temper, suggested to observers that the Middle Ages had come to an end. The papacy, the symbol of the spiritual unity of Christendom, had lost much of its prestige in the Great Schism (the period from 1378 to 1417 when there were two, and later three, rival popes); it also had become infected with the lay ideals of the Renaissance that were prevailing in the Italian peninsula. As the notion of a unified Christian realm foundered, the early modern period saw the rise of powerful nation-states, ruled by centralized monarchies, that vied for political dominance on the Continent.

At the same time, the papacy's spiritual supremacy was challenged by the Protestant Reformation, a reaction against the worldliness and corruption of the Roman Catholic Church. The Holy See responded in its turn by a revival of piety known as the Counter-Reformation. As the kingdoms of Europe variously sided with Protestantism or Roman Catholicism, these profound religious divisions were accompanied by widespread political turmoil.

THE STATE OF EUROPEAN POLITICS

As the emerging nation-states broke down local immunities and destroyed the unity of the European *respublica Christiana*, centralized bureaucracy came to replace medieval government. Secular values prevailed in politics, and the concept of a balance of power came to dominate international relations. Diplomacy and warfare were conducted by new methods. Permanent embassies were accredited between sovereigns, and on the battlefield standing armies of professional and mercenary soldiers took the place of the feudal array that had reflected the social structure of the past. Meanwhile, the narrow horizons of the Old World were widened by the expansion of Europe to America and the East.

DISCOVERY OF THE NEW WORLD

In the Iberian Peninsula the impetus of the counter-offensive against the Moors carried the Portuguese to probe the West African coastline and the Spanish to attempt the expulsion of Islam from the western Mediterranean. In the last years of the 15th century, Portuguese navigators established the sea route to India and within a decade had secured control of the trade routes in the Indian Ocean and its approaches. Mercantile interests, crusading and missionary zeal, and scientific curiosity were intermingled as the motives for this epic achievement. Similar hopes inspired Spanish exploitation of the discovery by Christopher Columbus of the Caribbean outposts of the American continent in 1492. The Treaties of Tordesillas and Saragossa in 1494 and 1529 defined the limits of westward Spanish exploration and the eastern ventures of Portugal. The two states acting as the vanguard of the expansion of Europe had thus divided the newly discovered sea lanes of the world between them.

By the time of the Treaty of Saragossa, when Portugal secured the exclusion of Spain from the East Indies, Spain had begun the conquest of Central and South America. In 1519, the year in which Ferdinand Magellan

In 1521, Portuguese explorer Ferdinand Magellan was killed in the Battle of Mactan, on an island that is now part of the Philippines. Archive Photos/ Getty Images

embarked on the westward circumnavigation of the globe, Hernán Cortés launched his expedition against Mexico. The seizure of Peru by Francisco Pizarro and the enforcement of Portuguese claims to Brazil completed the major steps in the Iberian occupation of the continent. By the middle of the century, the age of the conquistadores was replaced by an era of colonization, based both on the procurement of precious metal by Indian labour and on pastoral and plantation economies using imported African slaves. The influx of bullion into Europe became significant in the late 1520s, and from about 1550 it began to produce a profound effect upon the economy of the Old World.

NATION-STATES AND DYNASTIC RIVALRIES

The organization of expansion overseas reflected in economic terms the political nationalism of the European states. This political development took place through processes of internal unification and the abolition of local privileges by the centralizing force of dynastic monarchies. In Spain the union of Aragon, Valencia, and Catalonia under John II of Aragon was extended to association with Castile through the marriage of his son Ferdinand with the Castilian heiress Isabella. The alliance grew toward union after the accession of the two sovereigns to their thrones in 1479 and 1474, respectively, and with joint action against the Moors of Granada, the French in Italy, and the independent kingdom of Navarre. Yet, at the same time, provincial institutions long survived the dynastic union, and the representative assembly (Cortes) of Aragon continued to cling to its privileges when its Castilian counterpart had ceased to play any effective part. Castilian interest in the New World and Aragonese ties in Italy, moreover, resulted in the ambivalent nature of Spanish 16th-century policy, with its uneasy alternation between the Mediterranean and the Atlantic. The monarchy increased the central power by the absorption of military orders and the adaptation of the Hermandad, or police organization, and the Inquisition for political purposes. During the reign of Charles I (the emperor Charles V), centralization was quickened by the importation of Burgundian conciliar methods of government, and in the reign of his son Philip II, Spain was in practice an autocracy.

Other European monarchies imitated the system devised by Roman-law jurists and administrators in the Burgundian dominions along the eastern borders of France. In England and France the Hundred Years' War (conventionally 1337–1453) had reduced the strength of the aristocracies, the principal opponents of monarchical authority. The pursuit of strong, efficient government by the Tudors in England, following the example of their Yorkist predecessors, found a parallel in France under Louis XI and Francis I. In both countries revision of the administrative and judicial system proceeded through conciliar institutions, although in neither case did it result in the unification of different systems of law. A rising class of professional administrators came to fulfill the role of the king's executive. The creation of a central treasury under Francis I brought an order into French finances already achieved in England through Henry VII's adaptation of the machinery of the royal household. Henry VIII's minister, Thomas Cromwell, introduced an aspect of modernity into English fiscal administration by the creation of courts of revenue on bureaucratic lines. In both countries, the monarchy extended its influence over the government of the church. The unrestricted ability to make law was established by the English crown in partnership with Parliament. In France the representative Estates-General lost its authority, and sovereignty reposed in the king in council. Supreme courts (*parlements*) possessing the right to register royal edicts imposed a slight and ineffective limitation on the absolutism of the Valois kings. The most able exponent of the reform of the judicial machinery of the French monarch was Charles IX's chancellor, Michel de L'Hôpital, but his reforms in the 1560s were frustrated by the anarchy of the religious wars. In France the middle class aspired to ennoblement in the royal administration and mortgaged their future to the monarchy by investment in office and the royal finances. In England, on the other hand, a greater flexibility in social relations was preserved, and the middle class engaged in bolder commercial and industrial ventures.

Territorial unity under the French crown was attained through the recovery of feudal appanages (alienated to cadet branches of the royal dynasty) and, as in Spain, through marriage alliances. Brittany was regained in this way, although the first of the three Valois marriages with Breton heiresses also set in train the dynastic rivalry of Valois and Habsburg. When Charles VIII of France married Anne of Brittany, he stole the bride of the Austrian archduke and future emperor Maximilian I and also broke his own engagement to Margaret of Austria, Maximilian's daughter by Mary of Burgundy. Margaret's brother Philip, however, married Joan, heiress of Castile and Aragon, so that their son eventually inherited not only Habsburg Germany and the Burgundian Netherlands but also Spain, Spanish Italy, and America. The dominions of Charles V thus encircled France and incorporated the wealth of Spain overseas. Even after the division of this vast inheritance between his son, Philip II of Spain, and his brother, the emperor Ferdinand I, the conflict between the Habsburgs and the French crown dominated the diplomacy of Europe for more than a century.

The principal dynastic conflict of the age was less unequal than it seemed, for the greater resources of Charles V were offset by their cumbrous disunity and by local independence. In the Low Countries he was able to complete the Seventeen Provinces by new acquisitions, but, although the coordinating machinery of the Burgundian dukes remained in formal existence, Charles's regents were obliged to respect local privileges and to act through constitutional forms. In Germany, where his grandfather Maximilian I had unsuccessfully tried to reform the constitution of the Holy Roman Empire, Charles V could do little to overcome the independence of the lay and ecclesiastical princes, the imperial knights, and the free cities. The revolts of the knights (1522) and the peasantry (1525), together with the political disaggregation imposed by the Reformation, rendered the empire a source of weakness. Even in Spain, where the rebellion of the *comuneros* took place in 1520–21, his authority was sometimes flouted. His allies, England and the papacy, at times supported France to procure their own profit. France, for its part, possessed the advantages of internal lines of communication and a relatively compact territory, while its alliance with the Ottoman Empire maintained pressure on the Habsburg defenses in southeast Europe and the Mediterranean. Francis I, however, like his predecessors Charles VIII and Louis XII, made the strategic error of wasting his strength in Italy, where the major campaigns were fought in the first half of the century. Only under Henry II was it appreciated that the most suitable area for French expansion lay toward the Rhine.

TURKEY AND EASTERN EUROPE

A contemporary who rivaled the power and prestige of Francis I and Charles V was the ruler of the Ottoman

Charles V

(b. Feb. 24, 1500, Ghent [now in Belgium]—d. Sept. 21, 1558, San Jerónimo de Yuste, Spain)

Charles V, who reigned as Holy Roman emperor (1519–56) and king of Spain (as Charles I, 1516–56), inherited a Spanish and Habsburg empire that not only extended across Europe from Spain and the Netherlands to Austria and the Kingdom of Naples but also reached overseas to Spanish America. Son of Philip I of Castile and grandson of the Spanish monarchs Ferdinand V and Isabella I and of Holy Roman emperor Maximilian I, he succeeded to his grandfathers' kingdoms on their deaths in 1516 and 1519, respectively. Important events of his reign include the Diet of Worms and the beginning of the Reformation; his defeat of the French king Francis I, which assured Spanish supremacy in Italy; wars against Turkey under Süleyman I; the formation of the Schmalkaldic League; the Council of Trent; and the Peace of Augsburg. He struggled to hold his vast Spanish and Habsburg empire together against the growing forces of Protestantism, Turkish and French pressure, and even hostility from Pope Adrian VI. In 1555–56 Charles abdicated his claims to the Netherlands and Spain in favour of his son Philip II and the title of emperor to his brother Ferdinand I, and in 1557 he retired to a monastery in Spain.

In this painting, Holy Roman emperor Charles V of Spain, seated, looks at portraits with his son, Philip II. Hulton Archive/Getty Images

Empire, the sultan Süleyman I the Magnificent (1520–66). With their infantry corps d'élite (the Janissaries), their artillery, and their cavalry, or *sipahis*, the Ottomans were the foremost military power in Europe, and it was fortunate for their Christian adversaries that Eastern preoccupations prevented them from taking full advantage of Western disunity. A counterpoise was provided by the rise of the powerful military order of the Ṣafavids in Persia—hostile to the orthodox Ottomans through their acceptance of the heretical Islamic cult of the Shīʿites. Ottoman strength was further dissipated by the need to enforce the allegiance of Turkmen begs in Anatolia and of the chieftains of the Caucasus and Kurdistan and to maintain the conquest of the sultanate of Syria and Egypt by Süleyman's predecessor, Selim I. Süleyman himself overran Iraq and even challenged Portuguese dominion of the Indian Ocean from his bases in Suez and Basra. The Crimean Tatars acknowledged his suzerainty, as did the corsair powers of Algiers, Tunis, and Tripoli. His armies conquered Hungary in 1526 and threatened Vienna in 1529. With the expansion of his authority along the North African coast and the Adriatic littoral, it seemed for a time as if the Mediterranean, like the Black Sea and the Aegean, might become an Ottoman lake.

Though it observed the forms of an Islamic legal code, Turkish rule was an unlimited despotism, suffering from none of the financial and constitutional weaknesses of Western states. With its disciplined standing army and its tributary populations, the Ottoman Empire feared no internal threat except during the periods of disputed succession, which continued to occur despite a law empowering the reigning sultan to put to death collateral heirs. It was not unusual for the sultan to content himself with the overlordship of frontier provinces. Moldavia and Walachia were for a time held in this fashion, and in

Transylvania the *vaivode* (governor) John Zápolya gladly accepted Süleyman as his master in return for support against Ferdinand of Austria.

Despite the expeditions of Charles V against Algiers and Tunis, and the inspired resistance of Venice and Genoa in the war of 1537–40, the Ottomans retained the initiative in the Mediterranean until several years after the death of Süleyman. The Knights of St. John were driven from Rhodes and Tripoli and barely succeeded in retaining Malta. Even after Spain, the papacy, Venice, and Genoa had crushed the Turkish armament in 1571 in the Battle of Lepanto, the Ottomans took Cyprus and recovered Tunis from the garrison installed by the allied commander, Don John of Austria. North Africa remained an outpost of Islam and its corsairs continued to harry Christian shipping, but the Ottoman Empire did not again threaten Europe by land and sea until late in the 17th century.

Poland, Lithuania, Bohemia, and Hungary were all loosely associated at the close of the 15th century under rulers of the Jagiellon dynasty. In 1569, three years before the death of the last Jagiellon king of Lithuania-Poland, these two countries merged their separate institutions by the Union of Lublin. Thereafter the Polish nobility and the Roman Catholic faith dominated the Orthodox lands of Lithuania and held the frontiers against Muscovy, the Cossacks, and the Tatars. Bohemia and the vestiges of independent Hungary were regained by the Habsburgs as a result of dynastic marriages, which the emperor Maximilian I planned as successfully in the east as he did in the west. When Louis II of Hungary died fighting the Ottomans at Mohács in 1526, Archduke Ferdinand of Austria obtained both crowns and endeavoured to affirm the hereditary authority of his dynasty against aristocratic insistence on the principle of election. In 1619, Habsburg claims in Bohemia became the ostensible cause of the

Thirty Years' War, when the Diet of Prague momentarily succeeded in deposing Ferdinand II.

In the 16th century, eastern Europe displayed the opposite tendency to the advance of princely absolutism in the West. West of the Carpathians and in the lands drained by the Vistula and the Dnestr, the landowning class achieved a political independence that weakened the power of monarchy. The towns entered a period of decline, and the propertied class, though divided by rivalry between the magnates and the lesser gentry, everywhere reduced their peasantry to servitude. In Poland and Bohemia the peasants were reduced to serfdom in 1493 and 1497, respectively, and in free Hungary the last peasant rights were suppressed after the rising of 1514. The gentry, or *szlachta*, controlled Polish policy in the Sejm (parliament), and, when the first Vasa king, Sigismund III, tried to reassert the authority of the crown after his election in 1587, the opportunity had passed. Yet, despite the anarchic quality of Polish politics, the aristocracy maintained and even extended the boundaries of the state. In 1525 they compelled the submission of the secularized Teutonic Order in East Prussia, resisted the pressure of Muscovy, and pressed to the southeast, where communications with the Black Sea had been closed by the Ottomans and their tributaries.

Farther to the east the grand principality of Moscow emerged as a new and powerful despotism. Muscovy, and not Poland, became the heir to Kiev during the reign of Ivan III the Great in the second half of the 15th century. By his marriage with the Byzantine princess Sofia (Zoë) Palaeologus, Ivan also laid claim to the traditions of Constantinople. His capture of Novgorod and repudiation of Tatar overlordship began a movement of Muscovite expansion, which was continued by the seizure of Smolensk by his son Vasily (Basil) III and by the campaigns of his grandson Ivan IV the Terrible (1533–84). The latter destroyed the khanates of Kazan and Astrakhan and reached the Baltic by his conquest of Livonia from Poland and the Knights of the Sword. He was the first to use the title of tsar, and his arbitrary exercise of power was more ruthless and less predictable than that of the Ottoman sultan. After his death Muscovy was engulfed in the Time of Troubles, when Polish, Swedish, and Cossack armies devastated the land. The accession of the Romanov dynasty in 1613 heralded a period of gradual recovery. Except for occasional embassies, the importation of a few Western artisans, and the reception of Tudor trading missions, Muscovy remained isolated from the West. Despite its relationship with Greek civilization, it knew nothing of the Renaissance. Though it experienced a schism within its own Orthodox faith, it was equally untouched by Reformation and Counter-Reformation, the consequences of which convulsed western Europe in the late 16th century.

REFORMATION AND COUNTER-REFORMATION

In a sense, the Reformation was a protest against the secular values of the Renaissance. No Italian despots better represented the profligacy, the materialism, and the intellectual hedonism that accompanied these values than did the three Renaissance popes: Alexander VI, Julius II, and Leo X. Among those precursors of the reformers who were conscious of the betrayal of Christian ideals were figures so diverse as the Ferraran monk Savonarola, the Spanish statesman Cardinal Jiménez, and the humanist scholar Erasmus.

The corruption of the religious orders and the cynical abuse of the fiscal machinery of the church provoked

Süleyman I

(b. November 1494?/April 1495?—d. Sept. 5/6, 1566, near Szigetvár, Hung.)

The Ottoman sultan Süleyman I, called the Magnificent, ruled 1520–66. He became sultan of the Ottoman Empire after serving as a provincial governor under his grandfather Bayezid II and his father, Selim I (ruled 1512–20). He immediately began leading campaigns against the Christians, taking Belgrade (1521) and Rhodes (1522). At the Battle of Mohács (1526) he broke the military strength of Hungary. In 1529 he laid siege to Vienna but failed to capture it. Further campaigns in Hungary (1541, 1543) left the region divided between Habsburg- and Ottoman-dominated areas. Iraq and eastern Anatolia were captured during his first campaign (1534–35) against the Persian Ṣafavid dynasty; his second (1548–49) brought conquests in southern Anatolia around Lake Van; but his third (1554–55) was unsuccessful. His navy, under the Ottoman admiral Barbarossa, controlled the Mediterranean Sea. He built mosques, bridges, and aqueducts and surrounded himself with great poets and legal scholars. His reign is considered a high point of Ottoman civilization.

Ottoman sultan Süleyman I, the Magnificent. Time & Life Pictures/Getty Images

a movement that at first demanded reform from within and ultimately chose the path of separation. When the German priest Martin Luther protested against the sale of indulgences in 1517, he found himself obliged to extend his doctrinal arguments until his stand led him to deny the authority of the pope. In the past, as in the controversies between pope and emperor, such challenges had resulted in mere temporary disunity. In the age of nation-states, the political implications of the dispute resulted in the irreparable fragmentation of clerical authority.

Luther had chosen to attack a lucrative source of papal revenue, and his intractable spirit obliged Leo X to excommunicate him. The problem became as much concern to the emperor as it was to the pope, for Luther's eloquent writings evoked a wave of enthusiasm throughout Germany. The reformer was by instinct a social conservative and supported existing secular authority against the upthrust of the lower orders. Although the Diet of Worms accepted the excommunication in 1521, Luther found protection among German princes. In 1529 the rulers of electoral Saxony, Brandenburg, Hessen, Lüneberg, and Anhalt signed the "protest" against an attempt to enforce obedience. By this time, Holy Roman emperor Charles V had resolved to suppress Protestantism and to abandon conciliation. In 1527 his mutinous troops had sacked Rome and secured the person of Pope Clement VII, who had deserted the imperial cause in favour of Francis I after the latter's defeat at the Battle of Pavia. The sack of Rome proved a turning point both for the emperor and the humanist movement that he had patronized. The humanist scholars were dispersed, and the initiative for reform then lay in the hands of the more violent and uncompromising party. Charles V himself experienced a revulsion of conscience that placed him at the head of the Roman Catholic reaction. The empire he ruled in name

Martin Luther

(b. Nov. 10, 1483, Eisleben, Saxony [now in Germany]—d. Feb. 18, 1546, Eisleben)

The German priest Martin Luther sparked the Reformation. Luther studied philosophy and law before entering an Augustinian monastery in 1505. He was ordained two years later and continued his theological studies at the University of Wittenberg, where he became a professor of biblical studies. He was shocked by the corruption of the clergy on a trip to Rome in 1510 and was later troubled by doubts centring on fear of divine retributive justice. His spiritual crisis was resolved when he hit on the idea of justification by faith, the doctrine that salvation is granted as a gift through God's grace. He urged reform of the Roman Catholic Church, protesting the sale of indulgences and other abuses, and in 1517 he distributed to the archbishop of Mainz and several friends his Ninety-five Theses (according to legend, Luther nailed the theses to the door of the castle church in Wittenberg); the theses questioned Roman Catholic teaching and called for reform. In 1521 he was excommunicated by Pope Leo IX and declared an outlaw at the Diet of Worms. Under the protection of the elector of Saxony, Luther took refuge in Wartburg. There he translated the Bible into German; his superbly vigorous translation has long been regarded as the greatest landmark in the history of the German language. He later returned to Wittenberg, and in 1525 he married the former nun Katherine of Bora, with whom he raised five children. Though his preaching was the principal spark that set off the Peasants' War (1524–25), his vehement denunciation of the peasants contributed to their defeat. His break with Rome led to the founding of the Lutheran Church; the Lutheran confession of faith or, Augsburg Confession, was produced with Luther's sanction by Philipp Melanchthon in 1530. Luther's writings included hymns, a liturgy, and many theological works.

was now divided into hostile camps. The Catholic princes of Germany had discussed measures for joint action at Regensburg in 1524; in 1530 the Protestants formed a defensive league at Schmalkalden. Reconciliation was attempted in 1541 and 1548, but the German rift could no longer be healed.

Lutheranism laid its emphasis doctrinally on justification by faith and politically on the God-given powers of the secular ruler. Other Protestants reached different conclusions and diverged widely from one another in their interpretation of the sacraments. In Geneva, Calvinism enforced a stern moral code and preached the mystery of grace with predestinarian conviction. It proclaimed the separation of church and state, but in practice its organization tended to produce a type of theocracy. Huldrych Zwingli and Heinrich Bullinger in Zürich taught a theology not unlike John Calvin's but preferred to see government

Martin Luther faces Emperor Charles V at the Diet of Worms in 1521, after which he was condemned as a heretic. Hulton Archive/Getty Images

in terms of the godly magistrate. On the left wing of these movements were the Anabaptists, whose pacifism and mystic detachment were paradoxically associated with violent upheavals.

Lutheranism established itself in northern Germany and Scandinavia and for a time exercised a wide influence both in eastern Europe and in the west. Where it was not officially adopted by the ruling prince, however, the more militant Calvinist faith tended to take its place. Calvinism spread northward from the upper Rhine and established itself firmly in Scotland and in southern and western France. Friction between Rome and nationalist tendencies within the Catholic church facilitated the spread of Protestantism. In France the Gallican church was traditionally nationalist and antipapal in outlook, while in England the Reformation in its early stages took the form of the preservation of Catholic doctrine and the denial of papal jurisdiction. After periods of Calvinist and then of Roman Catholic reaction, the Church of England achieved a measure of stability with the Elizabethan religious settlement.

In the years between the papal confirmation of the Jesuit order in 1540 and the formal dissolution of the Council of Trent in 1563, the Roman Catholic Church responded to the Protestant challenge by purging itself of the abuses and ambiguities that had opened the way to revolt. Thus prepared, the Counter-Reformation embarked upon recovery of the schismatic branches of Western Christianity. Foremost in this crusade were the Jesuits, established as a well-educated and disciplined arm of the papacy by Ignatius Loyola. Their work was made easier by the Council of Trent, which did not, like earlier councils, result in the diminution of papal authority. The council condemned such abuses as pluralism, affirmed the traditional practice in questions of clerical marriage and the use of the Bible, and clarified doctrine on issues such as the nature of the Eucharist, divine grace, and justification by faith. The church thus made it clear that it was not prepared to compromise; and, with the aid of the Inquisition and the material resources of the Habsburgs, it set out to reestablish its universal authority. It was of vital importance to this task that the popes of the Counter-Reformation were men of sincere conviction and initiative who skillfully employed diplomacy, persuasion, and force against heresy. In Italy, Spain, Bavaria, Austria, Bohemia, Poland, and the southern Netherlands (the future Belgium), Protestant influence was destroyed.

DIPLOMACY IN THE AGE OF THE REFORMATION

This was a golden era for diplomats and international lawyers. To the network of alliances that became established throughout Europe during the Renaissance, the Reformation added confessional pacts. Unfortunately, however, the two systems were not always compatible. The traditional amity between Castile and England, for example, was fatally undermined when the Tudor dynasty embraced Protestantism after 1532; and the "auld alliance" between Scotland and France was likewise wrecked by the progress of the Reformation in Scotland after 1560. Moreover, in many countries, the confessional divisions of Christendom after Luther created powerful religious minorities who were prepared to look abroad for guarantees of protection and solidarity: for example, the English Catholics to Spain and the French, German, and Dutch Calvinists to England.

These developments created a situation of chronic political instability. On the one hand, the leaders of countries which themselves avoided religious fragmentation

Counter-Reformation

Also called the Catholic Reformation, or Catholic Revival, the Counter-Reformation comprised the Roman Catholic efforts directed in the 16th and early 17th centuries both against the Protestant Reformation and toward internal renewal. The Counter-Reformation took place during roughly the same period as the Protestant Reformation, actually (according to some sources) beginning shortly before Martin Luther's issuance of his Ninety-five Theses (1517).

Early calls for reform grew out of criticism of the worldly attitudes and policies of the Renaissance popes and many of the clergy. New religious orders and other groups were founded to effect a religious renewal—e.g., the Theatines, the Capuchins, the Ursulines, and especially the Jesuits. Later in the century, John of the Cross and Teresa of Ávila promoted the reform of the Carmelite order and influenced the development of the mystical tradition. Francis of Sales had a similar influence on the devotional life of the laity.

There was little significant papal reaction to the Protestants or to demands for reform from within the Roman Catholic Church before mid-century. Pope Paul III (reigned 1534–49) is considered to be the first pope of the Counter-Reformation. It was he who in 1545 convened the Council of Trent. The council, which met intermittently until 1563, responded emphatically to the issues at hand. Its doctrinal teaching was a reaction against the Lutheran emphasis on the role of faith and God's grace and against Protestant teaching on the number and nature of the sacraments. Disciplinary reforms attacked the corruption of the clergy. There was an attempt to regulate the training of candidates for the priesthood; measures were taken against luxurious living on the part of the clergy, the appointment of relatives to church office, and the absence of bishops from their dioceses. Prescriptions were given about pastoral care and the administration of the sacraments.

The Roman Inquisition, an agency established in 1542 to combat heresy, was more successful in controlling doctrine and practice than similar bodies in those countries where Protestant princes had more power than the Roman Catholic Church. Political and military involvement directed against Protestant growth is most clearly

St. Teresa of Ávila. Hulton Archive/Getty Images

reflected in the policies of Emperor Charles V and in those of his son Philip II, who was associated with the Spanish Inquisition.

Various theologians—especially the Jesuit Robert Bellarmine—attacked the doctrinal positions of the Reformers, but there was no one to rival the theological and moral engagement evident in the writings of Luther or the eloquence and passion characteristic of the works of John Calvin. Roman Catholics tended to emphasize the beliefs and devotional subjects that were under direct attack by the Protestants—e.g., the Real Presence of Christ in the Eucharist, the Virgin Mary, and St. Peter.

A major emphasis of the Counter-Reformation was an ongoing missionary endeavour in parts of the world that had been colonized by predominantly Roman Catholic countries. The work of such men as Francis Xavier and others in Asia and of missionaries in the New World was rewarded with millions of baptisms, if not true conversions. There were also attempts to reconvert areas of the world that had once been Roman Catholic—e.g., England and Sweden.

(such as Spain) were often unsure whether to frame their foreign policy according to confessional or political advantage. On the other hand, the foreign policy of religiously divided states, such as France, England, and the Dutch Republic, oscillated often and markedly because there was no consensus among the political elite concerning the correct principles upon which foreign policy should be based.

The complexity of the diplomatic scene called for unusual skills among the rulers of post-Reformation Europe. Seldom has the importance of personality in shaping events been so great. The quixotic temperaments and mercurial designs of even minor potentates exerted a disproportionate influence on the course of events. Nevertheless, behind the complicated interplay of individuals and events, two constants may be detected. First, statesmen and churchmen alike consistently identified politics and religion as two sides of the same coin. Supporters of the Bohemian rebellion of 1618, for example, frequently stated that "religion and liberty stand or fall together": that is, a failure to defend and maintain religious liberty would necessarily lead to the loss of political freedom. The position of Emperor Ferdinand II (1619–37) was exactly the same. "God's blessing cannot be received," he informed his subjects, "by a land in which prince and vassals do not both fervently uphold the one true Catholic faith."

These two views, precisely because they were identical, were totally incompatible. That their inevitable collision should have so often produced prolonged wars, however, was due to the second "constant": the desire of political leaders everywhere, even on the periphery of Europe, to secure a balance of power on the Continent favourable to their interests. It is scarcely surprising that, when any struggle became deadlocked, the local rulers should look about for foreign support; it is more noteworthy that their neighbours were normally ready and eager to provide it. Queen Elizabeth I of England (1558–1603) offered substantial support after 1585 to the Dutch rebels against Philip II and after 1589 to the Protestant Henry IV of France against his more powerful Catholic subjects; Philip II of Spain (1556–98), for his part, sent troops and treasure to the French Catholics, while his son Philip III (1598–1621) did the same for the German Catholics.

This willingness to assist arose because every court in Europe believed in a sort of domino theory, which argued that, if one side won a local war, the rest of Europe would inevitably be affected. The Spanish version of the theory was expressed in a letter from Archduchess Isabella, regent of the Spanish Netherlands, to her master Philip IV in 1623: "It would not be in the interests of Your Majesty to allow the Emperor or the Catholic cause to go down, because of the harm it would do to the possessions of Your Majesty in the Netherlands and Italy." Thus the religious tensions released by the Reformation eventually pitted two incompatible ideologies against each other; this in turn initiated civil wars that lasted 30 years (in the case of France and Germany) and even 80 years (in the Netherlands), largely because all the courts of Europe saw that the outcome of each confrontation would affect the balance of power for a decade, a generation, perhaps forever.

THE WARS OF RELIGION

Germany, France, and the Netherlands each achieved a settlement of the religious problem by means of war, and in each case the solution contained original aspects. In Germany the territorial formula of *cuius regio, eius religio* applied—that is, in each petty state the population had to conform to the religion of the ruler. In France, the Edict of Nantes in 1598 embraced the provisions of previous treaties and accorded the Protestant Huguenots toleration within the state, together with the political and military means of defending the privileges that they had exacted. The southern Netherlands remained Catholic and Spanish, but the Dutch provinces formed an independent Protestant federation in which republican and dynastic influences were nicely balanced. Nowhere was toleration accepted as a positive moral principle, and seldom was it granted except through political necessity.

There were occasions when the Wars of Religion assumed the guise of a supranational conflict between Reformation and Counter-Reformation. Spanish, Savoyard, and papal troops supported the Catholic cause in France against Huguenots aided by Protestant princes in England and Germany. In the Low Countries, English, French, and

German armies intervened; and at sea Dutch, Huguenot, and English corsairs fought the Battle of the Atlantic against the Spanish champion of the Counter-Reformation. In 1588 the destruction of the Spanish Armada against England was intimately connected with the progress of the struggles in France and the Netherlands.

Behind this ideological grouping of the powers, national, dynastic, and mercenary interests generally prevailed. The Lutheran duke Maurice of Saxony assisted Charles V in the first Schmalkaldic War in 1547 in order to win the Saxon electoral dignity from his Protestant cousin, John Frederick; while the Catholic king Henry II of France supported the Lutheran cause in the second Schmalkaldic War in 1552 to secure French bases in Lorraine. John Casimir of the Palatinate, the Calvinist champion of Protestantism in France and the Low Countries, maintained an understanding with the neighbouring princes of Lorraine, who led the ultra-Catholic Holy League in France. In the French conflicts, Lutheran German princes served against the Huguenots, and mercenary armies on either side often fought against the defenders of their own religion. On the one hand, deep divisions separated Calvinist from Lutheran; and, on the other hand, political considerations persuaded the moderate Catholic faction, the Politiques, to oppose the Holy League. The national and religious aspects of the foreign policy of Philip II of Spain were not always in accord. Mutual distrust existed between him and his French allies, the family of Guise, because of their ambitions for their niece Mary Stuart. His desire to perpetuate French weakness through civil war led him at one point to negotiate with the Huguenot leader, Henry of Navarre (afterward Henry IV of France). His policy of religious uniformity in the Netherlands alienated the most wealthy and prosperous part of his dominions. Finally, his ambition to make England and France the satellites of Spain weakened his ability to suppress Protestantism in both countries.

In 1562, seven years after the Peace of Augsburg had established a truce in Germany on the basis of territorialism, France became the centre of religious wars which endured, with brief intermissions, for 36 years. The political interests of the aristocracy and the vacillating policy of balance pursued by Henry II's widow, Catherine de Médicis, prolonged these conflicts. After a period of warfare and massacre, in which the atrocities of St. Bartholomew's Day (1572) were symptomatic of the fanaticism of the age, Huguenot resistance to the crown was replaced by Catholic opposition to the monarchy's policy of conciliation to Protestants at home and anti-Spanish alliances abroad. The revolt of the Holy League against the prospect of a Protestant king in the person of Henry of Navarre released new forces among the Catholic lower classes, which the aristocratic leadership was unable to control. Eventually Henry won his way to the throne after the extinction of the Valois line, overcame separatist tendencies in the provinces, and secured peace by accepting Catholicism. The policy of the Bourbon dynasty resumed the tradition of Francis I, and under the later guidance of Cardinal de Richelieu the potential authority of the monarchy was realized.

In the Netherlands the wise Burgundian policies of Charles V were largely abandoned by Philip II and his lieutenants. Taxation, the Inquisition, and the suppression of privileges for a time provoked the combined resistance of Catholic and Protestant. The house of Orange, represented by William I the Silent and Louis of Nassau, acted as the focus of the revolt; and, in the undogmatic and flexible personality of William, the rebels found leadership in many ways similar to that of Henry of Navarre. The sack of the city of Antwerp by mutinous Spanish soldiery in 1576 (three years after the dismissal of Philip II's autocratic and capable governor, the duque de Alba) completed the commercial decline of Spain's greatest economic asset. In 1579 Alessandro Farnese, duca di Parma, succeeded in recovering the allegiance of the Catholic provinces, while the Protestant north declared its independence. French and English intervention failed to secure the defeat of Spain, but the dispersal of the Armada and the diversion of Parma's resources to aid the Holy League in France enabled the United Provinces of the Netherlands to survive. A 12-year truce was negotiated in 1609, and when the campaign began again it merged into the general conflict of the Thirty Years' War, which, like the other wars of religion of this period, was fought mainly for confessional security and political gain.

CHAPTER 3

The Thirty Years' War, 1618–48

The war originated with dual crises at the Continent's centre: one in the Rhineland and the other in Bohemia, both part of the Holy Roman Empire.

"The dear old Holy Roman Empire,
How does it stay together?"

asked the tavern drinkers in Goethe's *Faust*—and the answer is no easier to find today. The Holy Roman Empire of the German Nation was a land of many polities. In the empire there were some 1,000 separate, semiautonomous political units, many of them very small, and others comparable in size with smaller independent states elsewhere, such as Scotland or the Dutch Republic. At the top came the lands of the Austrian Habsburgs, covering the elective kingdoms of Bohemia and Hungary, as well as Austria, the Tyrol, and Alsace, with about 8,000,000 inhabitants; next came electoral Saxony, Brandenburg, and Bavaria, with more than 1,000,000 subjects each; and then the Palatinate, Hesse, Trier, and Württemberg, with about 500,000 each.

These were large polities, indeed, but they were weakened by three factors. First, they did not accept primogeniture: Hesse, for instance, had been divided into four portions at the death of Landgrave Philip the Magnanimous in 1567. Second, many of the states were geographically fragmented. These factors had, in the course of time, created in Germany a balance of power between the states. The territorial strength of the Habsburgs may have brought them a monopoly of the imperial title from 1438 onward, but they could do no more: the other princes, when threatened, were able to form alliances whose military strength was equal to that of the emperor himself. However, the third weakness—the religious upheaval of the 16th century—changed all that: princes who had formerly stood together were now divided by religion. Swabia, for example, more or less equal in area to modern Switzerland, included 68 secular and 40 spiritual princes and also 32 imperial free cities. By 1618 more than half of these rulers were Catholic; the rest were Protestant.

THE CRISIS IN GERMANY

The Religious Peace of Augsburg in 1555 had put an end to 30 years of sporadic warfare in Germany between Catholics and Lutherans by creating a layered structure of legal securities in the empire. At the top was the right (*cuius regio, eius religio*) of every secular ruler to dictate whether their subjects' religion was to be Lutheran or Catholic (the only officially permitted creeds). The only exceptions to this rule were the imperial free cities, where both Lutherans and Catholics were to enjoy freedom of worship, and the Catholic ecclesiastical states, where bishops and abbots who wished to become Lutherans were obliged to resign first. The latter provision, known as the *reservatum ecclesiasticum*, gave rise to a war in 1583–88 when the archbishop of Cologne declared himself a Protestant but refused to resign: in the end a coalition of Catholic princes forced him out.

This "War of Cologne" was a turning point in the religious history of Germany. Until then, the Catholics had been losing ground steadily to the Protestants. After the successful struggle to retain Cologne, however, Catholic princes began to enforce the *cuius regio* principle with rigour. In Bavaria, as well as in Würzburg, Bamberg, and

Holy Roman Empire

A realm of varying extent in medieval and modern western and central Europe, the Holy Roman Empire traditionally is believed to have been established by Charlemagne, who was crowned emperor by Pope Leo III in 800. The empire lasted until the renunciation of the imperial title by Francis II in 1806. The reign of the German Otto I the Great (962–973), who revived the imperial title after Carolingian decline, is also sometimes regarded as the beginning of the empire. The name Holy Roman Empire (not adopted until the reign of Frederick I Barbarossa) reflected Charlemagne's claim that his empire was the successor to the Roman Empire and that this temporal power was augmented by his status as God's principal vicar in the temporal realm (parallel to the pope's in the spiritual realm).

The empire's core consisted of Germany, Austria, Bohemia, Moravia. Switzerland, the Netherlands, and northern Italy sometimes

Europe at the end of the Thirty Years' War. Courtesy of the University of Texas Libraries, The University of Texas at Austin

formed part of it; France, Poland, Hungary, and Denmark were initially included, and Britain and Spain were nominal components. From the mid-11th century the emperors engaged in a great struggle with the papacy for dominance, and, particularly under the powerful Hohenstaufen dynasty (1138–1208, 1212–54), they fought with the popes over control of Italy. Rudolf I became the first Habsburg emperor in 1273, and from 1438 the Habsburg dynasty held the throne for centuries.

Until 1356 the emperor was chosen by the German princes; thereafter, he was formally elected by the electors. At first there were seven electors: the archbishops of Trier, Mainz, and Cologne; the duke of Saxony; the count palatine of the Rhine; the margrave of Brandenburg; and the king of Bohemia. Other electorates were created later. Outside their personal hereditary domains, emperors shared power with the imperial diet.

During the Reformation the German princes largely defected to the Protestant camp, opposing the Catholic emperor. At the end of the Thirty Years' War, the Peace of Westphalia (1648) recognized the individual sovereignty of the empire's states; the empire thereafter became a loose federation of states and the title of emperor principally honorific. In the 18th century, issues of imperial succession resulted in the War of the Austrian Succession and the Seven Years' War. The greatly weakened empire was brought to an end in the early 19th century by the victories of Napoleon.

other ecclesiastical states, Protestants were given the choice of either conversion or exile. Most of those affected were adherents of the Lutheran church, already weakened by defections to Calvinism, a new creed that had scarcely a German adherent at the time of the Religious Peace of Augsburg. The rulers of the Palatinate (1560), Nassau (1578), Hesse-Kassel (1603), and Brandenburg (1613) all abandoned Lutheranism for the new confession, as did many lesser rulers and several towns. Small wonder that the Lutherans came to detest the Calvinists even more than they loathed the Catholics.

These religious divisions created a complex confessional pattern in Germany. By the first decade of the 17th
century, the Catholics were firmly entrenched south of
the Danube and the Lutherans northeast of the Elbe; but
the areas in between were a patchwork quilt of Calvinist,
Lutheran, and Catholic, and in some places one could find
all three. One such place was Donauwörth, an independent city just across the Danube from Bavaria, obliged
(by the Peace of Augsburg) to tolerate both Catholics and
Protestants. But for years the Catholic minority had not
been permitted full rights of public worship. When in
1606 the priests tried to hold a procession through the
streets, they were beaten and their relics and banners were
desecrated. Shortly afterward, an Italian Capuchin, Fray
Lorenzo da Brindisi, later canonized, arrived in the city
and was himself mobbed by a Lutheran crowd chanting
"Capuchin, Capuchin, scum, scum." He heard from the
local clergy of their plight and promised to find redress.
Within a year, Fray Lorenzo had secured promises of aid
from Duke Maximilian of Bavaria and Emperor Rudolf
II. When the Lutheran magistrates of Donauwörth flatly
refused to permit their Catholic subjects freedom of worship, the Bavarians marched into the city and restored
Catholic worship by force (December 1607). Maximilian's
men also banned Protestant worship and set up an occupation government that eventually transferred the city to
direct Bavarian rule.

These dramatic events thoroughly alarmed Protestants
elsewhere in Germany. Was this, they wondered, the first
step in a new Catholic offensive against heresy? Elector
Frederick IV of the Palatinate took the lead. On May 14,
1608, he formed the Evangelical, or Protestant, Union, an
association to last for 10 years, for self-defense. At first,
membership remained restricted to Germany, although
the elector's leading adviser, Christian of Anhalt, wished

to extend it, but before long a new crisis rocked the empire and turned the German union into a Protestant International.

The new crisis began with the death of John William, the childless duke of Cleves-Jülich, in March 1609. His duchies, occupying a strategic position in the Lower Rhineland, had both Protestant and Catholic subjects, but both of the main claimants to the inheritance were Protestants; under the *cuius regio* principle, their succession would lead to the expulsion of the Catholics. The emperor therefore refused to recognize the Protestant princes' claim. Since both were members of the Union, they solicited, and received, promises of military aid from their colleagues; they also received, via Christian of Anhalt, similar promises from the kings of France and England. This sudden accretion in Protestant strength caused the German Catholics to take countermeasures: a Catholic League was formed between Duke Maximilian of Bavaria and his neighbours on July 10, 1609, soon to be joined by the ecclesiastical rulers of the Rhineland and receiving support from Spain and the papacy. Again, reinforcement for one side provoked countermeasures. The Union leaders signed a defensive treaty with England in 1612 (cemented by the marriage of the Union's director, the young Frederick V of the Palatine, to the king of England's daughter) and with the Dutch Republic in 1613.

At first sight, this resembles the pyramid of alliances, patiently constructed by the statesmen of Europe 300 years later, which plunged the Continent into World War I. But whereas the motive of diplomats before 1914 was fear of political domination, before 1618 it was fear of religious extirpation. The Union members were convinced of the existence of a Catholic conspiracy aimed at rooting out all traces of Protestantism from the empire.

This view was shared by the Union's foreign supporters. At the time of the Cleves-Jülich succession crisis, Sir Ralph Winwood, an English diplomat at the heart of affairs, wrote to his masters that, although "the issue of this whole business, if slightly considered, may seem trivial and ordinary," in reality its outcome would "uphold or cast down the greatness of the house of Austria and the church of Rome in these quarters." Such fears were probably unjustified at this time. In 1609 the unity of purpose between pope and emperor was in fact far from perfect, and the last thing Maximilian of Bavaria wished to see was Habsburg participation in the League: rather than suffer it, in 1614 he formed a separate association of his own and in 1616 he resigned from the League altogether. This reduction in the Catholic threat was enough to produce reciprocal moves among the Protestants. Although there was renewed fighting in 1614 over Cleves-Jülich, the members of the Protestant Union had abandoned their militant stance by 1618, when the treaty of alliance came up for renewal. They declared that they would no longer become involved in the territorial wrangles of individual members, and they resolved to prolong their association for only three years more.

Although, to some extent, war came to Germany after 1618 because of the existence of these militant confessional alliances, the continuity must not be exaggerated. Both Union and League were the products of fear; but the grounds for fear seemed to be receding. The English ambassador in Turin, Isaac Wake, was sanguine: "The gates of Janus have been shut," he exulted in late 1617, promising "calm and Halcyonian days not only unto the inhabitants of this province of Italye, but to the greatest part of Christendome." That Wake was so soon proved wrong was due largely to events in the lands of the Austrian Habsburgs over the winter of 1617–18.

THE CRISIS IN THE HABSBURG LANDS

While the Cleves-Jülich crisis held the attention of western Europe in 1609, the eyes of observers farther east were on Prague, the capital of Bohemia. That elective kingdom (which also included Silesia, Lusatia, and Moravia), together with Hungary, had come to the Habsburg family in 1526. At first they were ruled jointly with Austria by Ferdinand I (brother of Emperor Charles V), but after his death in 1564 the inheritance was divided into three portions: Alsace and Tyrol (known as "Further Austria") went to one of his younger sons; Styria, Carinthia, and Carniola (known as "Inner Austria") went to a second; only the remainder was left for his successor as emperor, Maximilian II.

By 1609 fragmentation had advanced even further: Maximilian's eldest son, Rudolf II (emperor, 1576–1611), ruled only Bohemia; all the rest of his father's territories had been acquired, the previous year, by a younger son, Matthias. The new ruler had come to power not through strength or talent, however, but by the exploitation of the religious divisions of his subjects. During the 1570s the Protestants of Austria, Bohemia, and Hungary had used their strength of numbers and control of local representative assemblies to force the Habsburgs to grant freedom of worship to their Protestant subjects. This was clearly against the *cuius regio* principle, and everyone knew it. In 1599 the ruler of Inner Austria, Archduke Ferdinand, began a campaign of forcible re-Catholicization among his subjects, which proved entirely successful. But, when Rudolf II launched the same policy in Hungary shortly afterward, there was a revolt, and the rebels offered the Hungarian crown to Matthias in return for guarantees of toleration. The Bohemians decided to exploit Rudolf's temporary embarrassment by pressing him to grant similarly far-reaching concessions to the non-Catholic majority of that kingdom. The "Letter of Majesty" (Majestätsbrief) signed by Rudolf on July 9, 1609, granted full toleration to Protestants and created a standing committee of the Estates (nobles and representatives of the towns), known as "the Defensors," to ensure that the settlement would be respected.

Rudolf II—a recluse who hid in a world of fantasy and alchemy in his Hradčany palace above Prague, a manic depressive who tried to take his own life on at least one occasion—proved to be incapable of keeping to the same policy for long. In 1611 he tried to revoke the Letter of Majesty and to depose the Defensors by sending a small Habsburg army into Prague, but a force of superior strength was mobilized against the invaders, and the Estates resolved to depose Rudolf and offer their crown to Matthias. The emperor, broken in mind and body, died in January 1612. All his territories were then ruled by his brother, who also succeeded him as Holy Roman emperor later in the year. The alliance with the Protestant Estates that brought about Matthias's elevation, however, did not long continue once he was in power. The new ruler sought to undo the concessions he had made, and he looked for support to his closest Habsburg relatives: his brother Albert, ruler of the Spanish Netherlands; his cousin Ferdinand, ruler of Inner Austria; and his nephew Philip III, king of Spain. All three, however, turned him down.

Albert had in 1609 succeeded in bringing the war between Spain and the Dutch Republic to a temporary close with the Twelve Years' Truce. The last thing he wanted was to involve his ravaged country in supplying men and money to Vienna, perhaps provoking countermeasures from Protestants nearer home. Archduke Ferdinand, although willing to aid Matthias to uphold his authority (not least because he regarded himself as heir presumptive to the childless Matthias), was prevented from doing so by the outbreak of war between his Croatian subjects and the neighbouring republic of Venice (the Uskok War, 1615–18). Philip of Spain was also involved in war: in 1613–15 and 1616–17, Spanish forces in Lombardy fought the troops of the duke of Savoy over the succession to the childless duke of Mantua. Spain could therefore aid neither Matthias nor Ferdinand.

In 1617, however, papal diplomats secured a temporary settlement of the Mantuan question, and Spanish troops hastened to the aid of Ferdinand. Before long, Venice made overtures for peace, and the archduke was able to leave his capital at Graz in order to join Matthias. The emperor, old and infirm, was anxious to establish Ferdinand as his heir, and, in the autumn of 1617, the Estates of both Bohemia and Hungary were persuaded to recognize the archduke unconditionally as king-designate. On the strength of this, Ferdinand proceeded over the winter of 1617–18 to halt the concessions being made to Protestants. He created a council of regency for Bohemia that was overwhelmingly Catholic, and it soon began to censor works printed in Prague and to prevent non-Catholics from holding government office. More inflammatory still, the regents ordered Protestant worship to stop in towns on church lands (which they claimed were not included in the Letter of Majesty).

The Defensors created by the Letter of Majesty expressed strong objection to these measures and summoned the Estates of the realm to meet in May 1618. When the regents declared the meeting illegal, the Estates invaded the council chamber and threw two Catholic regents, together with their secretary, from the window. Next, a provisional government (known as the Directors) was created and a small army was raised.

In the Defenestration of Prague of 1618, Protestants threw two Catholic Regents out of a castle window. Although the governors were not seriously injured, this incident helped to ignite the Thirty Years' War. Kean Collection/ Hulton Archive/Getty Images

Apart from the famous "defenestration," the events in Prague in May 1618 were, superficially, little different from those in 1609 and 1611. Yet no 30-year struggle arose from those earlier crises. The crucial difference lay in the involvement of foreign powers: in 1609 and 1611 the Habsburgs, represented by Rudolf and Matthias, had given in to their subjects' demands; in 1618, led by Ferdinand, they did not. At first his defiant stance achieved nothing, for the army of the rebels expelled loyal troops from almost every part of the kingdom while their diplomats secured declarations of support from Silesia, Lusatia, and Upper Austria almost at once and from Moravia and Lower Austria shortly afterward. In May 1619 the rebel army even laid siege to Ferdinand in Vienna. Within weeks, however, they were forced to withdraw because a major Spanish army, partly financed by the pope, invaded Bohemia.

The appearance of Spanish troops and papal gold in eastern Europe immediately reawakened the fears of the Protestant rulers of the empire. To the government of Philip III, led by the former ambassador in Vienna, Don Balthasar de Zúñiga, the choice had seemed clear: "Your Majesty should consider," wrote one minister, "which will be of the greater service to you: the loss of these provinces [to the house of Habsburg], or the dispatch of an army of 15 to 20 thousand men to settle the matter." Seen in these terms, Spain could scarcely avoid military intervention in favour of Ferdinand; but to Protestant observers the logic of Spanish intervention seemed aggressive rather than defensive. Dudley Carleton, the English ambassador to the Dutch Republic, observed that the new emperor "flatters himself with prophesies of extirpating the Reformed religion and restoring the Roman church to the ancient greatness" and accurately predicted that, if the Protestant cause were to be "neglected and by consequence suppressed, the Protestant princes adjoining [Bohemia] are like to bear the burden of a victorious army."

This same argument carried weight with the director of the Protestant Union, Frederick V of the Palatinate, parts of whose territories adjoined Bohemia. So, when in the summer of 1619 the Bohemians deposed Ferdinand and offered the crown to Frederick, he was favourably disposed. Some of the elector's advisers favoured rejecting this offer, since "acceptance would surely begin a general religious war"; but others pointed out that such a war was inevitable anyway when the Twelve Years' Truce between Spain and the Dutch Republic expired in April 1621 and argued that allowing the Bohemian cause to fail would merely ensure that the conflict in the Netherlands would be resolved in Spain's favour later, making a concerted Habsburg attack on the Protestants of the empire both ineluctable and irresistible.

Frederick accepted the Bohemian crown and in so doing rekindled the worst fears of the German Catholics. The Catholic League was re-created, and in December 1619 its leaders authorized the levy of an army of 25,000 men to be used as Maximilian of Bavaria thought fit. At the same time, Philip III and Archduke Albert each promised to send a new army into Germany to assist Ferdinand (who had succeeded the late Matthias as Holy Roman emperor). The crisis was now apparent, and, as the Palatine diplomat Count John Albert Solms warned his master,

> *If it is true that the Bohemians are about to depose Ferdinand and elect another king, let everyone prepare at once for a war lasting twenty, thirty or forty years. The Spaniards and the House of Austria will deploy all their worldly goods to recover Bohemia.*

The underlying cause for the outbreak of a war that would last 30 years was thus the pathological fear of a Catholic conspiracy among the Protestants and the equally entrenched suspicion of a Protestant conspiracy among the Catholics. As a Bohemian noblewoman, Polyxena Lobkovic, perceptively observed from the vantage point of Prague: "Things are now swiftly coming to the pass where either the papists will settle their score with the Protestants, or the Protestants with the papists."

THE TRIUMPH OF THE CATHOLICS, 1619–29

Frederick V entered Prague and was crowned king by the rebel Estates in October 1619, but already the Catholic net was closing around him. The axis linking Vienna with Munich, Brussels, and Madrid enjoyed widespread support: subsidies came from Rome and Genoa, while

Tuscany and Poland sent troops. Equally serious, states favourable to Frederick's cause were persuaded to remain neutral: Spanish diplomacy kept England out of the war, while French efforts persuaded the Protestant Union to remain aloof from the Bohemian adventure of their leader. The Dutch Republic also did nothing, so that in the summer of 1620 a Spanish army was able to cross from the Netherlands and occupy the Rhine Palatinate. Meanwhile, the armies of the emperor and League, reinforced with Spanish and Italian contingents, invaded the rebel heartland. On November 8, in the first significant battle of the war, at the White Mountain outside Prague, Frederick's forces were routed. The unfortunate prince fled northward, abandoning his subjects to the mercy of the victorious Ferdinand.

This was total victory, and it might have remained the last word but for events in the Low Countries. Once the Twelve Years' Truce expired in April 1621, the Dutch, fearing a concerted attack by both Spanish and Austrian Habsburgs, decided to provide an asylum for the defeated Frederick and to supply diplomatic and, eventually, military assistance to his cause. In 1622 and again in 1623, armies were raised for Frederick with Dutch money, but they were defeated. Worse, the shattered armies retreated toward the Netherlands, drawing the Catholic forces behind them. It began to seem that a joint Habsburg invasion of the republic was inevitable after all.

The emperor's political position, however, weakened considerably in the course of 1623. Although his armies won impressive victories in the field, they were only able to do so thanks to massive financial and military support from the Catholic League, controlled by Maximilian of Bavaria. Ferdinand II, thanks to the Spanish and papal subsidies, maintained some 15,000 men himself, but the League provided him with perhaps 50,000. Thus Maximilian's armies had, in effect, won Ferdinand's victories and, now that all common enemies had been defeated, Maximilian requested his reward: the lands and electoral title of the outlawed Frederick of the Palatinate. Don Balthasar de Zúñiga, chief minister of Ferdinand's other major ally, Spain, warned that the consequences of acceding to this demand could be serious, but in October 1622 he died, and no one else in Madrid—least of all his successor as principal minister, the Count-Duke of Olivares—had practical experience of German affairs; so in January 1623 the emperor felt able to proceed with the investiture of Maximilian as elector Palatine.

Zúñiga, however, had been right: the electoral transfer provoked an enormous outcry, for it was clearly unconstitutional. The Golden Bull of 1356, which was universally regarded in Germany as the fundamental and immutable law of the empire, ordained that the electorate should remain in the Palatine house in perpetuity. The transfer of 1623 thus undermined a cornerstone of the Constitution, which many regarded as their only true safeguard against absolute rule. Inside Germany, a pamphlet war against Maximilian and Ferdinand began; outside, sympathy for Frederick at last created that international body of support for his cause which had previously been so conspicuously lacking. The Dutch and the Palatine exiles found little difficulty in engineering an alliance involving France, England, Savoy, Sweden, and Denmark that was dedicated to the restoration of Frederick to his forfeited lands and titles (the Hague Alliance, Dec. 9, 1624). Its leader was Christian IV of Denmark (1588–1648), one of the richest rulers in Christendom, who saw a chance to extend his influence in northern Germany under cover of defending "the Protestant cause." He invaded the empire in June 1625.

The Protestants' diplomatic campaign had not gone unnoticed, however. Maximilian's field commander, Count Tilly, warned that his forces alone would be no match for a coalition army and asked that the emperor send reinforcements. Ferdinand obliged: in the spring of 1625 he authorized Albrecht von Wallenstein, military governor of Prague, to raise an imperial army of 25,000 men and to move it northward to meet the Danish threat. Wallenstein's approach forced Christian to withdraw; when the Danes invaded again the following year, they were routed at the Battle of Lutter (Aug. 26, 1626). The joint armies of Tilly and Wallenstein pursued the defeated forces: first they occupied the lands of North German rulers who had declared support for the invasion, then they conquered the Danish mainland itself. Christian made peace in 1629, promising never again to intervene in the empire. His allies had long since withdrawn from the struggle.

Count Johann von Tilly. Rischgitz/Hulton Archive/Getty Images

The White Mountain delivered the Bohemian rebels into the emperor's grasp; Lutter delivered the rebels'
German supporters. After the victories, important new
policies were initiated by Ferdinand that aimed at exalt-
ing the Catholic religion and his own authority. In the
Habsburg provinces there was widespread confiscation
of land—perhaps two-thirds of the kingdom of Bohemia
changed hands during the 1620s—and a new class of loyal
landowners—like Wallenstein—was established. At the
same time, the power of the Estates was curtailed and freedom of worship for Protestants was restricted (in some
territories) or abolished (in most of the rest). Even a rebellion in Upper Austria in 1626, provoked principally by the
persecution of Protestants, failed to change Ferdinand's
mind. Indeed, fortified by his success in the Habsburg
lands, he decided to implement new policies in the
empire. First, disloyal rulers were replaced (the Palatinate
went to Maximilian, Mecklenburg to Wallenstein, and
so on). Next, serious steps were taken to reclaim church
lands that had fallen into Protestant hands. At first this
was done on a piecemeal basis, but on March 28, 1629, an
Edict of Restitution was issued which declared unilater-
ally that all church lands secularized since 1552 must be
returned at once, that Calvinism was an illegal creed in
the empire, and that ecclesiastical princes had the same
right as secular ones to insist that their subjects should
be of the same religion as their ruler. The last clause, at
least, was clearly contrary to the terms of the Peace of
Augsburg, which Protestants regarded as a central pillar
of the Constitution. There was, however, no opportunity
for argument, for the imperial edict was enforced immediately, brutally, by the armies of Wallenstein and Tilly,
which now numbered some 200,000 men. The people
of the empire seemed threatened with an arbitrary rule

against which they had no defense. It was this fear, skillfully exploited once again by Protestant propagandists, which ensured that the war in Germany did not end in 1629 with the defeat of Denmark. Ferdinand may have won numerous military victories, but in doing so he had suffered a serious political defeat. The pens of his enemies proved mightier than the sword.

THE CRISIS OF THE WAR, 1629–35

If Maximilian of Bavaria desired the title of elector as his reward for supporting Ferdinand, Spain (for its part) required imperial support for its war against the Dutch. When repeated requests for a direct invasion by Wallenstein's army remained unanswered (largely due to Bavarian opposition), Spain began to think of creating a Baltic navy, with imperial assistance, which would cleanse the inland sea of Dutch shipping and thus administer a body blow to the republic's economy. But the plan was aborted, for the imperial army failed in 1628 to conquer the port of Stralsund, selected as the base for the new fleet. Now, with Denmark defeated, Madrid again pleaded for the loan of an imperial army, and this time the request was granted. In the end, however, the troops did not march to the Netherlands: instead, they went to Italy.

The death of the last native ruler of the strategic states of Mantua and Montferrat in December 1627 created dangers in Italy that the Spaniards were unable to ignore and temptations that they were unable to resist. Hoping to forestall intervention by others, Spanish forces from Lombardy launched an invasion, but the garrisons of Mantua and Montferrat declared for the late duke's relative, the French-born duke of Nevers. Nevers lacked the resources to withstand the forces of Spain alone, and he appealed to France for support. Louis XIII (1610–43) and Cardinal de Richelieu (chief minister 1624–42) were, however, engaged in a desperate war against their Calvinist subjects; only when the rebels had been defeated, early in 1629, was it possible for the king and his chief minister to cross the Mount Cenis Pass and enter Italy. It was to meet this threat that the emperor was asked by Philip IV of Spain (1621–65) to send his troops to Italy rather than to the Netherlands. When Louis XIII launched a second invasion in 1630, some 50,000 imperial troops were brought south to oppose them, reducing the war for Mantua to a stalemate but delivering the Dutch Republic from immediate danger and weakening the emperor's hold on Germany.

Gustav II Adolf of Sweden (1611–32) had spent most of the 1620s at war with Poland, seeking to acquire territory on the southern shore of the Baltic. By the Truce of Altmark (Sept. 26, 1629), with the aid of French and British mediators, Poland made numerous concessions in return for a six-year truce. Gustav lost no time in redeploying his forces: on July 6, 1630, he led a Swedish expeditionary force ashore near Stralsund with the declared intention of saving the "liberties of the empire" and preserving the security of the Baltic.

Despite the defeat of the German Protestants and their allies, Sweden's position was far more favourable than that of Denmark five years earlier. Instead of the two armies that had faced Christian IV, Gustav was opposed by only one, for in the summer of 1630 the emperor's Catholic allies in Germany—led by Maximilian of Bavaria—demanded the dismissal of Wallenstein and the drastic reduction of his expensive army. It was an ultimatum that Ferdinand, with the bulk of his forces tied down in the war of Mantua, could not ignore, even though he thereby lost the services of the one man who might conceivably have retained all the imperial gains of the previous decade and united Germany under a strong monarchy.

The emperor and his German allies, nevertheless, did remain united over the Edict of Restitution: there were to be no concessions in matters of religion and no restoration of forfeited lands. As a result, the German Protestants were driven reluctantly into the arms of Sweden, whose army was increased with the aid of subsidies secured from France and the Dutch. In September 1631 Gustav at last felt strong enough to challenge the emperor's forces in battle: at Breitenfeld, just outside Leipzig in Saxony, he was totally victorious. The main Catholic field army was destroyed, and the Swedish Protestant host overran most of central Germany and Bohemia in the winter of 1631–32. The next summer they occupied Bavaria. Although Gustav died in battle at Lützen on Nov. 16, 1632, his forces were again victorious and his cause was directed with equal skill by his chief adviser, Axel Oxenstierna. In the east, Sweden managed to engineer a Russian invasion of Poland in the autumn of 1632 that tied down the forces of both powers for almost two years. Meanwhile, in Germany, Oxenstierna crafted a military alliance that transferred much of the cost of the war onto the shoulders of the German Protestant states (the Heilbronn League, April 23, 1633). Swedish ascendancy, however, was destroyed in 1634 when Russia made peace with Poland (at Polyanov, June 4) and Spain sent a large army across the Alps from Lombardy to join the imperial forces at the Battle of Nördlingen (September 6). This time the Swedes were decisively beaten and were obliged to withdraw their forces in haste from most of southern Germany.

Yet Sweden, under Oxenstierna's skillful direction, fought on. Certainly its motives included a desire to defend

This painting shows King Gustav II Adolf of Sweden leading Protestant forces at the Battle of Lützen (Germany), in 1632. His forces won this major battle of the Thirty Years' War, but he was killed leading a cavalry charge. Hulton Archive/Getty Images

the Protestant cause in Germany and to restore deposed princes to their thrones; but more important by far was the fear that if the German Protestants were finally defeated, the imperialists would turn the Baltic into a Habsburg lake and might perhaps invade Sweden. The Stockholm government therefore desired a settlement that would atomize the empire into a jumble of independent, weak states incapable of threatening the security of Sweden or its hold on the Baltic. Furthermore, to guarantee this fragmentation, Oxenstierna desired the transfer to his country of sovereignty over certain strategic areas of the empire—particularly the duchy of Pomerania on the Baltic coast and the electorate of Mainz on the Rhine.

These, however, were not at all the goals of Sweden's German allies. They aimed rather at the restoration of the prewar situation—in which there had been no place for Sweden—and it soon became clear that they were prepared to make a separate settlement with the emperor in order to achieve it. No sooner was Gustav dead than the elector of Saxony, as "foremost Lutheran prince of the Empire," put out peace-feelers toward Vienna. At first John George (1611–56) was adamant about the need to abolish the Edict of Restitution and to secure a full amnesty for all as preconditions for a settlement; but the imperial victory at Nördlingen made him less demanding. The insistence on an amnesty for Frederick V was dropped, and it was accepted that the edict would be applied in all areas recovered by Catholic forces before November 1627 (roughly speaking, this affected all lands south of the Elbe, but not the Lutheran heartland of Saxony and Brandenburg). The elector might have been required to make even more concessions but for the fact that, over the winter of 1634–35, French troops began to mass along the borders of Germany. As the papal nuncio in Vienna observed: "If the French intervene in Germany, the emperor will be forced to conclude peace with Saxony on whatever terms he can." So the Peace of Prague was signed between the emperor and the Saxons on May 30, 1635, and within a year most other German Lutherans also changed their allegiance from Stockholm to Vienna.

THE EUROPEAN WAR IN GERMANY, 1635–45

This partial settlement of the issues behind the war led many in Germany to look forward to a general peace. Certainly the exhaustion of many areas of the empire was a powerful incentive to end the war. The population of Lutheran Württemberg, for example, which was occupied by the imperialists between 1634 and 1638, fell from 450,000 to 100,000; material damage was estimated at 34 million thalers. Mecklenburg and Pomerania, occupied by the Swedes, had suffered in proportion. Even a city like Dresden, the capital of Saxony, which was neither besieged nor occupied, saw its demographic balance change from 121 baptisms for every 100 burials in the 1620s to 39 baptisms for every 100 burials in the 1630s. Amid such catastrophes an overwhelming sense of war-weariness engulfed Germany. The English physician William Harvey (discoverer of the circulation of blood), while visiting Germany in 1636, wrote:

> *The necessity they have here is of making peace on any condition, where there is no more means of making war and scarce of subsistence. . . . This warfare in Germany . . . threatens, in the end, anarchy and confusion.*

Attempts were made to convert the Peace of Prague into a general settlement. At a meeting of the electors held at Regensburg in 1636–37, Ferdinand II agreed to pardon any prince who submitted to him and promised to begin talks with the foreign powers to discover their terms for peace. But the emperor's death immediately after the meeting ended this initiative. Efforts by Pope Urban VIII (1623–44) to convene a general conference at Cologne were similarly unavailing. Then, in 1640, the new emperor, Ferdinand III (1637–57), assembled the Imperial Diet for the first time since 1613 in order to solve at least the outstanding German problems of the amnesty question and the restitution of church lands. He met with little success and could not prevent first Brandenburg (1641) and then Brunswick (1642) from making a separate agreement with

Sweden. The problem was that none of these attempts at peace were acceptable to France and Sweden, yet no lasting settlement could be made without them.

After the Peace of Prague, the nature of the Thirty Years' War was transformed. Instead of being principally a struggle between the emperor and his own subjects, with some foreign aid, it became a war of the emperor against foreign powers whose German supporters were, at most times, few in number and limited in resources. Sweden, as noted above, had distinct and fairly consistent war aims: to secure some bases in the empire, both as guarantees of influence in the postwar era and as some recompense for coming to the rescue of the Protestants, and to create a system of checks and balances in Germany, which would mean that no single power would ever again become dominant. If those aims could be achieved, Oxenstierna was prepared to quit. As he wrote:

> *We must let this German business be left to the Germans, who will be the only people to get any good out of it (if there is any), and therefore not spend any more men or money, but rather try by all means to wriggle out of it.*

But how could these objectives be best achieved? The Heilbronn League did not long survive the Battle of Nördlingen and the Peace of Prague, and so it became necessary to find an alternative source of support. The only one available was France. Louis XIII and Richelieu, fresh from their triumph in Italy, had been subsidizing Sweden's war effort for some time. In 1635, in the wake of Nördlingen, they signed an offensive and defensive alliance with the Dutch Republic (February 8), with Sweden (April 28), and with Savoy (July 11); they sent an army into the Alps to occupy the Valtelline, a strategic military link between the possessions of the Spanish and Austrian Habsburgs (March); and they mediated a 20-year truce between Sweden and Poland (September 12). Finally, on May 19, 1635, they declared war on Spain.

The aims of France were very different from those of Sweden and its German allies. France wished to defeat Spain, its rival for more than a century, and its early campaigns in Germany were intended more to prevent Ferdinand from sending aid to his Spanish cousins than to impose a Bourbon solution on Germany—indeed, France only declared war on Ferdinand in March 1636. Sweden at first therefore avoided a firm commitment to France, leaving the way clear for a separate peace should the military situation improve sufficiently to permit the achievement of its own particular aims. The war, however, did not go in favour of the allies. French and Swedish forces, operating separately, totally failed to reverse the verdict of Nördlingen: despite the Swedish victory at Wittstock (Oct. 4, 1636) and French gains in Alsace and the middle Rhine (1638), the Habsburgs always seemed able to even up the score. Thus in 1641 Oxenstierna abandoned his attempt to maintain independence and threw in his lot with France. By the terms of the Treaty of Hamburg (March 15, 1641), the two sides promised not to make a separate peace. Instead, joint negotiations with the emperor and the German princes for the satisfaction of the allies' claims were to begin in the Westphalian towns of Münster and Osnabrück. And, while the talks proceeded, the war was to continue.

The Treaty of Hamburg had at last created a coalition capable of destroying the power both of Ferdinand III and of Maximilian of Bavaria. On the whole, France attacked Bavaria, and Sweden fought the emperor; but there was considerable interchange of forces and a carefully coordinated strategy. On Nov. 2, 1642, the Habsburgs' army was routed in Saxony at the Second Battle of Breitenfeld, and the emperor was saved from further defeat only by the outbreak of war between Denmark and Sweden (May 1643–August 1645). Yet, even before Denmark's final surrender, the Swedes were back in Bohemia, and at Jankov (March 6, 1645) they totally destroyed another imperial army. The emperor and his family fled to Graz, while the Swedes advanced to the Danube and threatened Vienna. Reinforcements were also sent to assist the French campaign against Bavaria, and on August 3 Maximilian's forces were decisively defeated at Allerheim.

Jankov and Allerheim were two of the truly decisive battles of the war, because they destroyed all possibility of the Catholics obtaining a favourable peace settlement. In September 1645 the elector of Saxony made a separate peace with Sweden and so—like Brandenburg and Brunswick before him—in effect withdrew from the war. Meanwhile, at the peace conference in session in Westphalia, the imperial delegation began to make major concessions: Oxenstierna noted with satisfaction that, since Jankov, "the enemy begins to talk more politely and pleasantly." He was confident that peace was just around the corner. He was wrong.

MAKING PEACE, 1645–48

One hundred and ninety-four European rulers, great and small, were represented at the Congress of Westphalia, and talks went on constantly from the spring of 1643 until the autumn of 1648. The outstanding issues of the war were solved in two phases: the first, which lasted from November 1645 until June 1647, saw the chief imperial negotiator, Maximilian, Count Trauttmannsdorf, settle most issues; the second, which continued from then until the treaty of peace was signed in October 1648, saw France try to sabotage the agreements already made.

The purely German problems were resolved first, partly because they were already near solution and partly because the foreign diplomats realized that it was best (in the words of Count d'Avaux, the French envoy)

> *to place first on the table the items concerning public peace and the liberties of the Empire, ... because if the German rulers do not yet truly wish for peace, it would be ... damaging to us if the talks broke down over our own particular demands.*

So in 1645 and 1646, with the aid of French and Swedish mediation, the territorial rulers were granted a large degree of sovereignty (*Landeshoheit*), a general amnesty was issued to all German princes, an eighth electorate was created for the son of Frederick V (so that both he and Maximilian possessed the coveted dignity), the Edict of Restitution was finally abandoned, and Calvinism within the empire was granted official toleration. The last two points were the most bitterly argued and led to the division of the German rulers at the Congress into two blocs: the Corpus Catholicorum and the Corpus Evangelicorum. Neither was monolithic or wholly united, but eventually the Catholics split into those who were prepared to make religious concessions in order to have peace and those who were not. A coalition of Protestants and pragmatic Catholics then succeeded in securing the acceptance of a formula that recognized as Protestant all church lands in secular hands by Jan. 1, 1624 (that is, before the gains made by Wallenstein and Tilly), and granted freedom of worship to religious minorities where these had existed by the same date. The Augsburg settlement of 1555 was thus entirely overthrown, and it was agreed that any change to the new formula must be achieved only through the "amicable composition" of the Catholic and Protestant blocs, not by a simple majority.

The amicable composition principle was finally accepted by all parties early in 1648, thus solving the last German problem. That this did not lead to immediate peace was due to the difficulty of satisfying the foreign powers involved. Apart from France and Sweden, representatives from the Dutch Republic, Spain, and many other non-German participants in the war were present, each of them eager to secure the best settlement they could. The war in the Netherlands was the first to be ended: on Jan. 30, 1648, Philip IV of Spain signed a peace that recognized the Dutch Republic as independent and agreed to liberalize trade between the Netherlands and the Iberian world. The French government, led since Richelieu's death (Dec. 4, 1642) by Jules Cardinal Mazarin (Giulio Mazzarino), was bitterly opposed to this settlement, since it left Spain free to deploy all its forces in the Low Countries against France; as a consequence, France devoted all its efforts to perpetuating the war in Germany. Although Mazarin had already signed a preliminary agreement with the emperor in September 1646, which conveyed parts of Alsace and Lorraine to France, in 1647-48 he started a new campaign in Germany in order to secure more. On May 17, 1648, another Bavarian army was destroyed at Zusmarshausen, near Nördlingen, and Maximilian's lands were occupied by the French.

Mazarin's desire to keep on fighting was thwarted by two developments. On the one hand, the pressure of the war on French taxpayers created tensions that in June 1648 erupted into the revolt known as the Fronde. On the other hand, Sweden made a separate peace with the emperor. The Stockholm government, still directed by Oxenstierna, was offered half of Pomerania, most of Mecklenburg, and the secularized bishoprics of Bremen and Verden; it was to receive a seat in the Imperial Diet; and the territories of the empire promised to pay five million thalers to the Swedish army for its wage arrears. With so many tangible gains, and with Germany so prostrated that there was no risk of any further imperial attack, it was clearly time to wriggle out of the war, even without France; peace was thus signed on August 6.

Without Sweden, Mazarin realized that France needed to make peace at the earliest opportunity. He informed his representatives at the Congress:

It is almost a miracle that . . . we can keep our affairs going, and even make them prosper; but prudence dictates that we should not place all our trust in this miracle continuing for long.

Mazarin therefore settled with the emperor on easy terms: France gained only the transfer of a bundle of rights and territories in Alsace and Lorraine and little else. Mazarin could, nevertheless, derive satisfaction from the fact that, when the ink dried on the final treaty of Oct. 24, 1648, the emperor was firmly excluded from the empire and was under oath to provide no further aid to Spain. Mazarin settled down to suppress the Fronde revolt and to win the war against Philip IV.

PROBLEMS NOT SOLVED BY THE WAR

Some historians have sought to diminish the achievements of the Thirty Years' War, and the peace that ended it, because not all of Europe's outstanding problems

This 2007 photo shows archaeologists uncovering a mass grave of soldiers from the Thirty Years' War near Wittstock, Germany. Approximately 7,000 people died in a battle between Swedish and Saxon troops on Oct. 4, 1636. Michael Urban/AFP/Getty Images

were settled. The British historian C.V. Wedgwood, for example, in a classic study of the war first published in 1938, stated baldly:

> *The war solved no problem. Its effects, both immediate and indirect, were either negative or disastrous. . . . It is the outstanding example in European history of meaningless conflict.*

It is true that the struggle between France and Spain continued with unabated bitterness until 1659 and that within a decade of the Westphalian settlement, Sweden was at war with Poland (1655–60), Russia (1656–58), and Denmark (1657–58). It is also true that in the east, a war broke out in 1654 between Poland and Russia that was to last until 1667, while tension between the Habsburgs and the Turks increased until war came in 1663. Even within the empire, there were disputes over the partition of Cleves-Jülich, still a battle zone after almost a half-century, which caused minor hostilities in 1651. Lorraine remained a theatre of war until the duke signed a final peace with France in 1661. But to expect a single conflict in early modern times to have solved all of Europe's problems is anachronistic: the Continent was not the single political system that it later became. It is wrong to judge the Congress of Westphalia by the standard of the Congress of Vienna (1815). Examined more closely, the peace conference that ended the Thirty Years' War settled a remarkable number of crucial issues.

PROBLEMS SOLVED BY THE WAR

The principal Swedish diplomat at Westphalia, Johann Adler Salvius, complained to his government in 1646 that

> *people are beginning to see the power of Sweden as dangerous to the balance of power. Their first rule of politics here is that the security of all depends upon the equilibrium of the individuals. When one ruler begins to become powerful . . . the others place themselves, through unions or alliances, into the opposite balance in order to maintain the equipoise.*

It was the beginning of a new order in Europe, and Sweden, for all her military power, was forced to respect it. The system depended on channeling the aggression of German princes from thoughts of conquering their neighbours to dreams of weakening them; and it proved so successful that, for more than a century, the settlement of 1648 was widely regarded as the principal guarantee of order and peace in central Europe. In 1761 Jean-Jacques Rousseau wrote in praise of the "balance of power" in

Europe which, he believed, was anchored in the constitution of the Holy Roman Empire,

> *which takes from conquerors the means and the will to conquer. . . . Despite its imperfections, this Imperial constitution will certainly, while it lasts, maintain the balance in Europe. No prince need fear lest another dethrone him. The peace of Westphalia may well remain the foundation of our political system for ever.*

As late as 1866, the French statesman Adolphe Thiers claimed that

> *Germany should continue to be composed of independent states connected only by a slender federative thread. That was the principle proclaimed by all Europe at the Congress of Westphalia.*

It was indeed: the balance of power with its fulcrum in Germany, created by the Thirty Years' War and prolonged by the Peace of Westphalia, was a major achievement. It may not have lasted, as Rousseau rashly prophesied, forever, but it certainly endured for more than a century.

It was, for example, almost a century before German rulers went to war with each other again—a strong contrast with the hundred years before 1618, which had been full of armed neutrality and actual conflict. The reason for the contrast was simple: the Thirty Years' War had settled both of the crises which had so disturbed the peace in the decades before it began.

In the lands of the Austrian Habsburgs, there were now no powerful Estates and no Protestant worship (except in Hungary), and, despite all the efforts of the Swedish diplomats at Westphalia, there was no restoration of the lands confiscated from rebels and others. The Habsburg Monarchy, born of disparate units but now entirely under the authority of the king-emperor, had become a powerful state in its own right. Purged of political and religious dissidents and cut off from its western neighbours and from Spain, the compact private territories of the Holy Roman emperor were still large enough to guarantee him a place among the foremost rulers of Europe. In the empire, by contrast, the new stability rested upon division rather than unity. Although the territorial rulers had acquired, at Westphalia, supreme power in their localities and collective power in the Diet to regulate common taxation, defense, laws, and public affairs without imperial intervention, the "amicable composition" formula prevented in fact any changes being made to the status quo. The originality of this compromise (enshrined in Article V, paragraph 52, of the Instrumentum Pacis Osnabrugense) has not always been appreciated. An age that normally revered the majority principle sanctioned an alternative method—parity between two unequal groups (known as *itio in partes*)—for reaching decisions.

Looked at more pragmatically, what the *itio in partes* formula achieved was to remove religion as a likely precipitant of political conflict. Although religion remained a matter of high political importance (for instance, in cementing an alliance against Louis XIV after 1685 or in unseating James II of England in 1688), it no longer determined international relations as it once had done.

When one of the diplomats at the Congress of Westphalia observed that "reason of state is a wonderful animal, for it chases away all other reasons," he in fact paid tribute to the secularization that had taken place in European politics since 1618. But when, precisely, did it happen? Perhaps with the growing preponderance of non-German rulers among the enemies of the emperor.

Without question, those German princes who took up arms against Ferdinand II were strongly influenced by confessional considerations, and, as long as these men dominated the anti-Habsburg cause, so too did the issue of religion. Frederick of the Palatine and Christian of Anhalt, however, failed to secure a lasting settlement. Gradually the task of defending the Protestant cause fell into the hands of Lutherans, less militant and less intransigent than the Calvinists; and the Lutherans were prepared to ally, if necessary, with Anglican England, Catholic France, and even Orthodox Russia in order to create a coalition capable of defeating the Habsburgs. Naturally such states had their own reasons for fighting; and, although upholding the Protestant cause may have been among them, it seldom predominated. After 1625, therefore, the role of religious issues in European politics steadily receded. This was, perhaps, the greatest achievement of the war, for it thus eliminated the major destabilizing influence in European politics, which had both undermined the internal cohesion of many states and overturned the diplomatic balance of power created during the Renaissance.

CHAPTER 4

EUROPEAN SOCIETY AND ECONOMY, C. 1648–1788

By the 17th century there was already a tradition and awareness of Europe: a reality stronger than that of an area bounded by sea, mountains, grassy plains, steppes, or deserts where Europe clearly ended and Asia began—"that geographical expression," which in the 19th century Otto von Bismarck was to see as counting for little against the interests of nations. In the two centuries before the French Revolution and the triumph of nationalism as a divisive force, Europe exhibited a greater degree of unity than appeared on the mosaic of its political surface. With appreciation of the separate interests that Bismarck would identify as "real" went diplomatic, legal, and religious concerns which involved states in common action and contributed to the notion of a single Europe. King Gustav II Adolf of Sweden saw one aspect when he wrote: "All the wars that are afoot in Europe have become as one."

A European identity took shape in the work of Hugo Grotius, whose *De Jure Belli et Pacis* (1625; *On the Law of War and Peace*) was a plea for the spirit of law in international relations. It gained substance in the work of the great congresses (starting with those of Münster and Osnabrück before the Peace of Westphalia in 1648) that met not only to determine rights and frontiers, taking into account the verdict of battle and resources of states, but also to settle larger questions of justice and religion. By 1700 statesmen had begun to speak of Europe as an interest to be defended against the ambitions of particular states. Europe represented an audience for those who wrote about the great issues of faith, morals, politics, and, increasingly, science: René Descartes did not write only for Frenchmen, nor Gottfried Wilhelm Leibniz for Germans. The use of Latin as the language of diplomacy and scholarship and the ubiquity, alongside local systems and customs, of Roman law were two manifestations of the unity of Christendom.

As a spiritual inheritance and dynamic idea greater than the sum of the policies of which it was composed, "Christendom" best represents Europe as envisaged by those who thought and wrote about it. The existence of vigorous Jewish communities—at times persecuted, as in Poland in 1648, but in places such as Amsterdam secure, prosperous, and creative—only serves to emphasize the essential fact: Europe and Christendom remained inter-changeable terms. The 16th century had experienced schism, and the development of separate confessions had shredded "the seamless robe," but it had done so without destroying the idea of catholicism to which the Roman church gave institutional form. The word *catholic* survived in the creeds of Protestant churches, such as that of England. John Calvin had thought in catholic, not sectarian, terms when he mourned for the Body of Christ, "bleeding, its members severed." Deeper than quarrels about articles of belief or modes of worship lay the mentality conditioned by centuries of war against pagan and infidel, as by the Reconquista in Spain, which had produced a strong idea of a distinctive European character. The Renaissance, long-evolving and coloured by local conditions, had promoted attitudes still traceable to the common inheritance. The Hellenic spirit of inquiry, the Roman sense of order, and the purposive force of Judaism had contributed to a cultural synthesis and within

This 17th-century portrait of a rabbi was painted by Dutch painter Rembrandt van Rijn. Imagno/Hulton Archive/Getty Images

it an article of faith whose potential was to be realized in the intellectual revolution of the 17th century—namely, that man was an agent in a historical process which he could aspire both to understand and to influence.

By 1600 the outcome of that process was the complex system of rights and values comprised in feudalism, chivalry, the crusading ideal, scholasticism, and humanism. Even to name them is to indicate the rich diversity of the European idea, whether inspiring adventures of sword and spirit or imposing restraints upon individuals inclined to change. The forces making for change were formidable. The Protestant and Roman Catholic Reformations brought passionate debate of an unsettling kind. Discoveries and settlement overseas extended mental as well as geographic horizons, brought new wealth, and posed questions about the rights of indigenous peoples and Christian duty toward them. Printing gave larger scope to authors of religious or political propaganda. The rise of the state brought reactions from those who believed they lost by it or saw others benefit exceedingly from new sources of patronage.

Meanwhile, the stakes were raised by price inflation, reflecting the higher demand attributable to a rise in the population of about 25 percent between 1500 and 1600 and the inflow of silver from the New World; the expansion of both reached a peak by 1600. Thereafter, for a century, the population rose only slightly above 100 million and pulled back repeatedly to that figure, which seemed to represent a natural limit. The annual percentage rate of increase in the amount of bullion in circulation in Europe, which had been 3.8 in 1550 and 1 in 1600, was, by 1700, 0.5. The extent to which these facts, with attendant phenomena—notably the leveling out from about 1620, and thereafter the lowering, of demand, prices, and rents before the resumption of growth about 1720—influenced the course of events

must remain uncertain. Controversy has centred around
the cluster of social, political, and religious conflicts and
revolts that coincided with the deepening of the recession toward mid-century. Some historians have seen there
not particular crises but a "general crisis." Most influential in the debate have been the Marxist view that it was
a crisis of production and the liberal political view that it
was a general reaction to the concentration of power at
the centre.

Any single explanation of the general crisis may be
doomed to fail. That is not to say that there was no connection between different features of the period. These
arose from an economic malaise that induced an intro-
spective mentality, which tended to pessimism and led
to repressive policies but which also was expressed more
positively in a yearning and search for order. So appear
rationalists following Descartes in adopting mathematical principles in a culture dominated by tradition; artists
and writers accepting rules such as those imposed by
the French Academy (founded 1635); statesmen looking
for new principles to validate authority; economic theo-
rists (later labeled "mercantilists") justifying the need to
protect and foster native manufactures and fight for an
apparently fixed volume of trade; the clergy, Catholic and
Protestant alike, seeking uniformity and tending to persecution; witch-hunters rooting out irregularities in the
form of supposed dealings with Satan; even gardeners trying to impose order on unruly nature. Whether strands
in a single pattern or distinct phenomena that happen to
exhibit certain common principles, each has lent itself to a
wider perception of the 17th century as classical, baroque,
absolutist, or mercantilist.

There is sufficient evidence from tolls, rents, taxes,
riots, and famines to justify arguments for something
more dire than a downturn in economic activity. There

are, however, other factors to be weighed: prolonged wars fought by larger armies, involving more matériel, and having wider political repercussions; more efficient states, able to draw more wealth from taxpayers; and even, at certain times (such as the years 1647–51), particularly adverse weather, as part of a general deterioration in climatic conditions. There are also continuities that cast doubt on some aspects of the general picture. For example, the drive for conformity can be traced at least to the Council of Trent, whose final sessions were in 1563; but it was visibly losing impetus, despite Louis XIV's intolerant policy leading to the revocation of the Edict of Nantes (1685), after the Peace of Westphalia. Puritanism, which has been seen as a significant reflection of a contracting economy, was not a prime feature of the second half of the century, though mercantilism was. Then there are exceptions even to economic generalizations: England and, outstandingly, the United Provinces of the Netherlands. Insights and perspectives gain from the search for general causes. But truth requires an untidy picture of Europe in which discrepancies abound, in which men subscribe to a common civilization while cherishing specific rights; in which countries evolved along distinctive paths; and in which much depended on the idiom of a community, on the ability of ruler or minister, on skills deployed and choices made.

Complementing the search for order and for valid authority in other fields, and arising out of the assertion of rights and the drive to control, a feature of the 17th century was the clarification of ideas about the physical bounds of the world. In 1600 "Europe" still lacked exact political significance. Where, for example, in the eastern plains before the Ural Mountains or the Black Sea were reached, could any line have meaning? Were Christian peoples—Serbs, Romanians, Greeks, or Bulgarians—living under Turkish rule properly Europeans? The tendency everywhere was to envisage boundaries in terms of estates and lordships. Where the legacy of feudalism was islands of territory either subject to different rulers or simply independent, or where, as in Dalmatia or Podolia (lands vulnerable to Turkish raids), the frontier was represented by disputed, inherently unstable zones, a linear frontier could emerge only out of war and diplomacy. The process can be seen in the wars of France and Sweden. Both countries were seen by their neighbours as aggressive, yet they were concerned as much with a defensible frontier as with the acquisition of new resources. Those objectives inspired the expansionist policies of the French ministers Richelieu and Mazarin and King Louis XIV and—with the added incentives of fighting the infidel and recovering a patrimony lost since the defeat at Mohács in 1526—the reconquest of Hungary, which led to the Treaty of Carlowitz (1699). The frontier then drawn was sufficiently definite—despite modifications, as after the loss of Belgrade (1739)—to make possible effective government within its perimeter.

Another feature of the period was the drawing into the central diplomatic orbit of countries that had been absorbed hitherto in questions of little consequence. Although Henry of Valois had been elected king of Poland before he inherited the French throne (1574) and James VI of Scotland (later James I of England, 1603–25) had married Anne of Denmark, whose country had a footing in Germany through its duchy of Holstein, it was still usual for western statesmen to treat the Baltic states as belonging to a separate northern system. Trading interests and military adventures that forged links, for example, with the United Provinces—as when Sweden intervened in the German war in 1630—complicated already tangled diplomatic questions.

Travelers who ventured beyond Warsaw, Kraków, and the "black earth" area of Mazovia, thence toward the

Pripet Marshes, might not know when they left Polish lands and entered those of the tsar. The line between Orthodox Russia and the rest of Christian Europe had never been so sharp as that which divided Christendom and Islam. Uncertainties engendered by the nature of Russian religion, rule, society, and manners perpetuated former ambivalent attitudes toward Byzantium. Unmapped spaces, where Europe petered out in marshes, steppes, and forests of birch and alder, removed the beleaguered though periodically expanding Muscovite state from the concern of all but neighbouring Sweden and Poland. The establishment of a native dynasty with the accession of Michael Romanov in 1613, the successful outcome of the war against Poland that followed the fateful revolt in 1648 of Ukraine against Polish overlordship, the acquisition of huge territories including Smolensk and Kiev (Treaty of Andrusovo, 1667), and, above all, the successful drive of Peter I the Great to secure a footing in the Baltic were to transform the picture. By the time of Peter's death in 1725, Russia was a European state: still with some Asian characteristics, still colonizing rather than assimilating southern and eastern lands up to and beyond the Urals, but interlocked with the diplomatic system of the West. A larger Europe, approximating to the modern idea, began to take shape.

THE HUMAN CONDITION

For most inhabitants of Europe, the highest aim was to survive in a hazardous world. They were contained in an inelastic frame by their inability to produce more than a certain amount of food or to make goods except by hand or by relatively simple tools and machines. In this natural, or preindustrial, economy, population played the main part in determining production and demand through

99

the amount of labour available for field, mill, and work-shop and through the number of consumers. Jean Bodin (writing toward the end of an age of rising population) stated what was to become the truism of the anxious 17th century when he wrote that men were "the only strength and wealth." The 16th century had seen the last phase in recovery from the Black Death, which had killed about a third of Europe's people. The 1590s brought a sharp check: dearth and disorder were especially severe in France and Spain. There were particular reasons: the effect of civil wars and Spanish invasion in France, the load placed on the Castilian economy by the imperialist policies of Philip II. France made a speedy, if superficial, recovery during the reign of Henry IV, but the truce between Spain and the United Provinces (1609) presented the Dutch with an open market from which they proceeded to drive out the native producers. Meanwhile, virulent outbreaks of plague had contributed to Spain's loss of more than a million people.

A feature of the late 16th century had been the growth of cities. Those that had flourished most from expansion of trade or government offered sustenance of a kind for refugees from stricken villages. Meanwhile, peasants were paying the price for the intensified cultivation necessitated by the 16th century's growth in population. The subdivision of holdings, the cultivation of marginal land, and the inevitable preference for cereal production at the cost of grazing, with consequent loss of the main fertilizer, animal dung, depressed crop yields. The nature of the trap that closed around the poor can be found in the statistics of life expectancy, averaging 25 years but nearer 20 in the larger towns. It took three times as many births to maintain the level of population as it did at the end of the 20th century.

There also were large fluctuations, such as that caused by the loss of at least 5 of Germany's 20 million during the Thirty Years' War. The "vital revolution" is an apt description of the start of a process that has continued to the present day. Until 1800, when the total European population was about 180 million, growth was modest and uneven: relatively slow in France (from 20 to 27 million), Spain (from 7 to 9 million), and Italy (from 13 to 17 million) and nonexistent in war-torn Poland until 1772, when the first of three partitions anticipated its demise as a political entity. Significantly, the rise in population was the most marked in Britain, where agriculture, manufacturing, and trade benefited from investment and innovation, and in Russia, which was technologically backward but which colonized near-empty lands. Among the causes were improvements in housing, diet, and hygiene.

CLIMATE

Given people's dependence on nature, the deterioration of the climate during the Little Ice Age of the 17th century should be considered as a demographic factor. The absence of sunspots after 1645 was noted by astronomers using the recently invented telescope; the aurora borealis (caused by high-energy particles from the Sun entering the Earth's atmosphere) was so rarely visible that it was thought ominous when it did appear; measurement of tree rings shows them to be relatively thin in this period but containing heavy deposits of radioactive carbon-14, associated with the decline of solar energy; snow lines were observed to be lower; and glaciers advanced into Alpine valleys, reaching their farthest point about 1670. All of these phenomena support plentiful anecdotal evidence for a period of unfavourable climate characterized by cold winters and wet summers. A decrease of about 1 percent in solar radiation meant a growing season shorter by three weeks and the altitude at which crops would ripen lowered by about 500 feet (150 metres). With most of the population living near subsistence level and depending upon cereal crops, the effect was most severe on those who farmed marginal land, especially on northerners for whom the growing season was already short. They were not the only ones who suffered, for freakish conditions were possible then as now. Around Toledo—where until the late 17th century the plains and sierras of New Castile provided a bare living from wheat, vines, and olives— disastrous frosts resulted in mass emigration. Drought also brought deprivation. During 1683 no rain fell in Andalusia until November; the cattle had to be killed, the crops were dry stalks, and thousands starved. In the great winter of 1708–09, rivers froze, even the swift-flowing Rhône, and wolves roamed the French countryside; after late frosts, which killed vines and olive trees, the harvest was a catastrophe: by December the price of bread had quadrupled.

Less spectacular, but more deadly, were the sequences of cold springs and wet summers. From the great mortalities such as those of 1647–52 and 1691–95 in France the population was slow to recover; women were rendered infertile, marriages were delayed, and births were avoided. They were times of fear for masters and shameful resort to beggary, abortion, and infanticide for the common people. It was also a hard time for the government and its tax-collectors. The disastrous harvest of the previous year was the direct cause of the revolt of the Sicilians in 1648. The connection between the outbreak of France's Fronde revolt in the same year and harvest failure is less direct: some revolt would probably have occurred in any case. There is a clear link, however, between the wet Swedish summer of 1649 and the constitutional crisis of the following year.

WAR

The period between the revolt of Bohemia (1618) and the peace of Nystad (1721), which coincides with the check to growth and subsequent recession, also saw prolonged warfare. Developments within states and leagues between them made possible the mustering of larger armies than ever before. How important then was war as an influence on economic and social conditions? The discrepancy between the high aspirations of sovereigns and the brutal practice of largely mercenary soldiers gave the Thirty Years' War a nightmarish character. It is, however, hard to be precise about the consequences of this general melee. As hostilities ended, rulers exaggerated losses to strengthen claims for compensation; refugees returned, families emerged from woods and cellars and reappeared on tax rolls; ruined villages were rebuilt and wastelands were tilled; a smaller population was healthier and readily procreative. The devastation was patchy. Northwestern Germany, for example, was little affected; some cities, such as Hamburg, actually flourished, while others, such as Leipzig and Nürnberg, quickly responded to commercial demand. The preindustrial economy proved to be as resilient as it was vulnerable. Yet the German population did not rise to prewar levels until the end of the 17th century.

The causes of this demographic disaster lie in the random nature of operations and the way in which armies, disciplined only on the battlefield, lived off the land. Casualties in battle were not the prime factor. In the warfare of the 17th and 18th centuries, mortal sickness in the armies exceeded death in action in the proportion of five to one. Disease spread in the camps and peasant communities deprived by pillage of their livelihood. The cost to the home country of operations abroad could be comparatively small, as it was to Sweden, at least until 1700 and the Great Northern War, which developed into a struggle for survival. Special factors—notably naval and commercial strength, the ability to prey on the enemy's commerce and colonies, and immigration from the occupied south—enabled the United Provinces to grow richer from their wars against Spain (1572–1609 and 1621–48). By contrast, those living in the main theatres of war and occupation were vulnerable: the Spanish southern provinces of the Netherlands, Lorraine (open to French troops), Pomerania and Mecklenberg (to Swedish troops), and Württemberg (to Austrian and French) were among those who paid the highest bills of war.

The ability of states to bring their armies under control meant that operations after 1648 were better regulated and had less effect on civilians. Lands were ravaged deliberately to narrow a front or to deprive the enemy of base and food: such was the fate of the Palatinate, sacked by the French under Marshall René Tessé in 1689. Meanwhile, warfare in the north and east continued to be savage, largely unrestrained by conventions that were gaining hold in the west. The war of the Spanish Succession (1701–14) ran parallel with the Great Northern War (1700–21) and the war of Austria (allied with Venice and sometimes Poland) against the Turks, which had begun with the relief of Vienna in 1683 and continued intermittently until the peace of Passarowitz in 1718. In brutal campaigning over the plains of Poland and Hungary, the peasants were the chief sufferers. For the Hungarians, long inured to border war, liberation by the Habsburgs meant a stricter landowning regime. In one year, 1706, the Swedes gutted 140 villages on the estates of one of Augustus II's followers. The Russians never subscribed to the stricter rules that were making western warfare look like a deadly game of chess. The later years of Frederick the Great were largely devoted to the restoration of Prussia, despoiled during the Russian occupation of 1760–62.

Such exceptions apart, it seems that most people were little affected by military operations after 1648. The Flemish peasant plowed the fields in peace within miles of the encampments of the English general John Churchill, duke of Marlborough; his uniformed troops received regular pay and looting was punished. That was the norm for armies of the 18th century. This improvement was a factor in the rise of population in that century, but not the main one. At worst, war only exacerbated the conditions of an underdeveloped society.

HEALTH AND SICKNESS

By the dislocation of markets and communications and the destruction of shipping, and by diverting toward destructive ends an excessive proportion of government funds, war tended to sap the wealth of the community and narrow the scope for governments and individuals to plan and invest for greater production. The constructive reforms of the French statesman Jean-Baptiste Colbert in the 1660s, for example, would have been unthinkable in the 1640s or '50s; they were checked by the renewal of war after 1672 and were largely undone by the further sequence of wars after his death. War determined the evolution of states, but it was not the principal factor affecting the lives of people. Disease was ever present, ready to take advantage of feeble defense systems operating without the benefit of science. The 20th-century French historian Robert Mandrou wrote of "the chronic morbidity" of the entire population. There is plenty of material on diseases, particularly in accounts of symptoms and "cures," but the language is often vague. Christian of Brunswick was consumed in 1626 "by a gigantic worm"; Charles II of

Spain, dying in 1700, was held to be bewitched; men suffered from "the falling sickness" and "distemper."

There are no reliable statistics about height and weight. It is difficult even to define what people regarded as normal good health. The average person was smaller than today. Even if courtiers flattered Louis XIV, deemed to be tall at 5 feet 4 inches (1.6 metres), the evidence of portraits and clothes shows that a Frenchman of 6 feet (1.8 metres) was exceptionally tall; the same goes for most southern and central Europeans. Scandinavians, Dutch, and North Germans were generally larger; protein in meat, fish, and cheese was probably as important as their ethnic stock. Even where there were advances in medicine, treatment of illness remained primitive. The majority who relied on the simples or charms of the local wise woman may have been no worse off than those for whom more learned advice was available. Court doctors could not prevent the

About 1630, English physician William Harvey, who discovered the circulation of the blood, demonstrates his theories to King Charles I. Hulton Archive/Getty Images

death of the duc de Bourgogne, his wife, and his eldest son in 1712 from what was probably scarlet fever; the younger son, the future Louis XV, may have been saved by his nurse's removing him from their ministrations.

The work of William Harvey, concerning the circulation of the blood; of Antonie van Leeuwenhoek, observing through his microscope blood circulating in minute capillaries or spermatozoa in water; of Francesco Redi, developing by experiment (in a book of 1668) Harvey's principle that "all living things come from an egg"; or of Hermann Boerhaave, professor of chemistry, medicine, and botany at Leiden, carrying out public dissections of human bodies, reveals the first approaches to modern knowledge and understanding. A striking example of what could be achieved was the efficacy of vaccine against the rampant smallpox after the discoveries of Edward Jenner and others, but vaccination was not much used until the beginning of the 19th century. As in other scientific fields, there was a long pause between pioneering research and regular practice. Trained by book, taking no account of organic life, envisaging illness as a foreign element lodged in the sick person's body, even tending to identify disease with sin, doctors prescribed, dosed, and bled, leaning on pedantic scholarship blended with primitive psychology. Therapy was concerned mainly with moderating symptoms. For this purpose mercury, digitalis, ipecac root, and, especially, opium were used; the latter was addictive but afforded relief from pain. The wisest navigators in this frozen sea were those who knew the limitations of their craft, like William Cullen, an Edinburgh physician who wrote: "We know nothing of the nature of contagion that can lead us to any measures for removing or correcting it. We know only its effects."

To peer in imagination into the hovels of the poor or to walk down streets with open drains between houses decayed into crowded tenements, to visit shanty towns outside the walls, such as London's Bethnal Green or Paris's Faubourg Saint-Marcel, to learn that the latter city's great open sewer was not covered until 1740, is to understand why mortality rates among the poor were so high. In town and country they lived in one or two rooms, often under the same roof as their animals, sleeping on straw, eating with their fingers or with a knife and spoon, washing infrequently, and tolerating lice and fleas. Outside, dung and refuse attracted flies and rodents. Luckier people, particularly in the north, might have had glass in their windows, but light was less important than warmth. In airless rooms, thick with the odours of dampness, defecation, smoke, and unwashed bodies, rheumatic or bronchial ailments might be the least of troubles. Deficient diet in childhood could mean rickety legs. Crude methods of delivery might cause permanent damage to both mothers and children who survived the attentions of the local midwife. The baby who survived (one in four died in the first year of life) was launched on a hazardous journey.

Some diseases, such as measles, seem to have been more virulent then than now. Typhus, spread by lice and fleas, and typhoid, waterborne, killed many. Tuberculosis was less common than it was to become. Cancer, though hard to recognize from contemporary accounts, was certainly rare: with relatively little smoking and with so many other diseases competing for the vulnerable body, that is not surprising. There were few illnesses, mental or physical, of the kind today caused by stress. Alcoholism was less common, despite the increase in the drinking of spirits that debauched city dwellers: cheap gin became a significant social problem in William Hogarth's London. Abnormalities resulting from inbreeding were frequent in mountain valleys or on remote coasts.

Syphilis had been a growing menace since its introduction in the 16th century, and it was rife among prostitutes and their patrons: it was a common cause of blindness in children. Women, hapless victims of male-dominated morality, were frequently denied the chance of early mercury treatment because of the stigma attached to the disease. Scrofula, a gangrenous tubercular condition of the lymph glands, was known as "the king's evil" because it was thought to be curable by the king's touch: Louis XIV practiced the ceremony conscientiously. Malaria was endemic in some swampy areas. Though drainage schemes were taken up by enlightened sovereigns, prevention awaited inexpensive quinine. Nor could doctors do more than let smallpox take its course before the general introduction of vaccines. The plague, chiefly an urban disease that was deadliest in summer and dreaded as a sentence of death, could be combated only by measures of quarantine such as those enforced around Marseille in 1720, when it made its last appearance in France. Its last European visitation was at Messina in 1740. Deliverance from plague was not the least reason for Europeans of the Enlightenment to believe that they were entering a happier age.

POVERTY

Though its extent might vary with current economic trends, poverty was a constant state. It is hard to define since material expectations vary among generations, social groups, and countries. If those with sufficient land or a wage large enough to allow for the replacement of tools and stock are held to be above the poverty line, then at least a quarter of Europe's inhabitants were below it. They were the *bas peuple* whom the French engineer Sébastien Le Prestre de Vauban observed in the 1690s, "three-fourths of them . . . dressed in nothing

but half-rotting, tattered linen"; a century later the philosopher the marquis de Condorcet described those who
"possess neither goods nor chattels [and are] destined to
fall into misery at the least accident." That could be illness
or injury to a breadwinner, the failure of a crop or death
of a cow, fire or flood, or the death or bankruptcy of an
employer. Sometimes poverty showed itself in a whole
community demoralized through sickness—as by malaria
in Italy's Pontine Marshes and goitre in Alpine valleys—or
through the sapping of vitality when the young left to find
work. Factors could be the unequal struggle with a poor
soil or the exactions of a landowner: so the agricultural
writer Arthur Young, at Combourg, wondered that the
seigneur, "this Monsieur de Chateaubriant, . . . has nerves
strung for such a residence amidst such filth and poverty."
Many were victims of an imprisoning socioeconomic
regime, such as Castilian latifundia or Polish serfdom. A
trade depression, a change of fashion, or an invention that
made traditional manufacturing obsolete could bring destitution to busy cities such as Leiden, Lyon, Florence, or
Norwich or to specialized communities such as the silk
weavers of 18th-century England's Spitalfields.

Taxes, on top of rents and dues, might be the decisive factor in the slide from sufficiency to destitution.
A member of the Castilian Cortes of 1621 described the
results: "Numerous places have become depopulated and
disappeared from the map. . . . The vassals who formerly
cultivated them now wander the roads with their wives
and children." Some had always been beyond the reach of
the collector of taxes and rents, such as the *bracchianti* (day
labourers) described by a Mantuan doctor as "without a
scrap of land, without homes, lacking everything except
a great brood of children . . . with a humble train of a few
sheep and baggage consisting of a tattered bedstead, a
mouldy cask, some rustic tools and a few pots and pans."

Moneylenders were pivotal figures in village society. In southern Italy, merchants advanced money on wheat in *contratti alla voce* (oral agreements). The difference between the arranged price and that at harvest time, when the loan was repaid, represented their profit. Throughout Europe, land changed hands between lender and borrower: foreclosure and forfeit is an aspect of primitive capitalism often overlooked in the focus on trade and manufacturing. Society, even in long-settled areas, revealed a constant flux. As the 20th-century French historian Marc Bloch pointed out, hierarchy was always present in some degree, even in districts where sharecropping meant dependence on the owner's seed and stock. In the typical village of western Europe, there were gradations between the well-to-do farmer, for whom others worked and whose strips would grow if he continued to be thrifty, and the day labourer, who lived on casual labour, hedging, ditching, thatching, repairing terraces, pruning vines, or making roads.

Urban poverty posed the biggest threat to governments. The situation became alarming after 1750 because the rise in population forced food prices up, while the employers' advantage in the labour market depressed wages. Between 1730 and 1789, living costs in France rose by 62 percent; in Germany the price of rye for the staple black bread rose by up to 30 percent while wages fell. In Italian cities the poor depended on the authorities' control of markets, prices, and food supplies. The riots of Genoa in 1746 show what was liable to happen if they failed. The causes of riots varied. In England, in 1766, grievances included the Irish, Roman Catholics, the press-gang, and gin taxes. The source was almost invariably poverty measured against a vague conception of a "fair wage," fanned by rumours about hoarding and the creating of false prices. Paris was not uniquely dangerous. Before 1789, when the fury of the mob acquired political importance, the Gordon

Riots (1780) had shown the way in which London could be taken over by a mob. The problem originated in rural poverty. Improvements in agriculture, such as enclosure, did not necessarily provide more work. Where there were no improvements or old abuses continued—such as the short-term leases of southern Italy, which encouraged tenants to over-crop and so exhaust the soil—the city provided the only hope. Naples, with the greatest profusion of beggars in the streets, was the most swollen of cities: at 438,000 in 1797, the population had risen by 25 percent in 30 years.

The typical relationship of mutual support was between poor hill country and large town; Edinburgh or Glasgow provided support for the Scots Highlanders, Vienna or Marseille for the Alpine poor. In Marseille a settled population of 100,000 supported 30,000 immigrants. Younger sons from the European fringes went for bread to the big armies: Croats to the Austrian, Finns to the Swedish, Scots and Irish everywhere. Women were usually left behind with the old men and children to look after the harvest in areas of seasonal migration. Domestic service drew many girls to towns with a large bourgeois population. Certain other occupations, notably lacemaking, were traditionally reserved for women. Miserably paid, young Frenchwomen risked their eyesight in fine work to earn enough for dowry and marriage. In a society where contraception was little known, except through abstinence, and irregular liaisons were frowned upon, the tendency to marry late was an indication of poverty. Almost half the women of western Europe married after 25; between 10 and 15 percent did not marry at all. The prevalence of abortion and infanticide is painfully significant: it was clearly not confined to unmarried couples. In 18th-century Brussels, more than 2,000 babies were abandoned annually to be looked after by charitable institutions. Repairs to a drain in Rennes in the 1720s revealed the tiny skeletons of 50 babies. Every major city had large numbers of prostitutes. There were approximately 20,000 in Paris, and, more surprisingly, in staid, episcopally governed Mainz, it was estimated that a third of the women in the poorer districts were prostitutes. Victims and outcasts, with the beggars and derelicts of crowded tenements, they helped create the amoral ambience in which criminals could expect tolerance and shelter.

Naturally associated with poverty, crime was also the product of war, even the very maintenance of armies. Desertion led to a man's living an outlaw's life. Despite ferocious penalties (having the nose and one ear cut off) the Prussian army lost 30,000 deserters between 1713 and 1740. The soldier's life might not equip a man for settled work. It was hard, in unsettled times, to distinguish between overtly treasonous acts, as of leaders in revolts, and the persistent banditry that accompanied and outlasted them. Another gray area surrounded the arbitrary actions of officials—for example, billeting troops, sometimes, as in the *dragonnades* employed by Louis XIV against the Huguenots, for political reasons. Tax collection often involved violence and chicanery. The notorious Mandrin, whose prowess Tobias Smollett recorded, had also been a tax collector. Leader of a gang of some 500, he used his knowledge of the system to construct a regime of extortion. Eventually betrayed and broken on the wheel, he remained a local hero.

Banditry was a way of life on the Cossack and Balkan marches, but it was not only there that roads were unsafe. Barred by magistrates from the towns, gangs of beggars terrorized country districts. Children, pursuing victims with sorry tales, were keen trainees in the school of crime, picking pockets, cutting horsetails, soliciting for "sisters," and abetting smuggling. The enlargement of the role of the state, with tariffs as the main weapon in protectionist strategies, encouraged evasion and smuggling. Just as few country districts were without robbers, few coasts were without smuggling gangs. A Norman seaman could make more by one clandestine Channel crossing than by a year's fishing. Only the approval of the poor could make romantic figures of such criminals as Dick Turpin or Marion de Fouet.

The savagery of punishments was in proportion to the inadequacy of enforcement. To traditional methods— hanging, dismemberment, flogging, and branding—the possession of colonies added a new resort toward the end of the 18th century, that of transportation. By then, notably in the German and Italian lands of the Habsburg brothers Joseph II and Leopold II, who were influenced by arguments of reason and humanity, crime was fought at the source by measures to liberate trade, moderate punishments, and increase provision for the poor.

A central theme in Christian teaching was the blessed state of the poor. Holy poverty was the friars' ideal; ardent reformers ensured that some returned to it. The ascetic Father Joseph, personal agent of Cardinal de Richelieu, and Abraham Sancta Clara, preacher at the court of Leopold I, were representative figures. With the acceptance of poverty went awareness of a Christian's duty to relieve it. Alms for the poor figured largely in wills and were a duty of most religious orders. Community charity had a larger place in Counter-Reformation Catholicism than in the thinking of Protestants, who stressed private virtues and endowments. The secularization of church property that accompanied the Reformation reduced levels of relief. However, meticulous church elders in Holland and parish overseers in England were empowered to raise poor rates. In Brandenburg a law of 1696 authorized parishes to provide work for the deserving poor and punishment for others. In Denmark the government pronounced in 1683 that the pauper had the legal right to relief: he could work in land reclamation or road building. Different was the

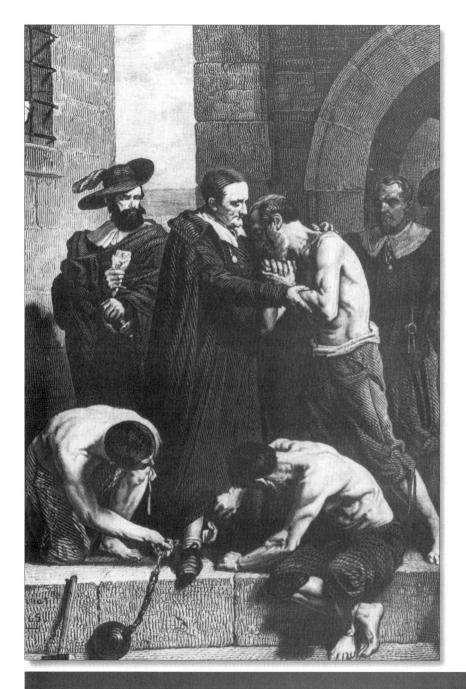

This painting of St. Vincent de Paul shows him sacrificing himself by taking the place of a group of suffering galley slaves. Hulton Archive/Getty Images

approach of Vincent de Paul (1581–1660), whose instructions to the Sisters of Charity, founded to help "our lords
the poor," were both compassionate and practical. His idea
of the *hôpital général*, a privately funded institution for the
aged, crippled, and orphaned, was taken over in 1662: an
edict commended the institution of *hôpitaux* throughout
the land. Care for the poor was tinged with concern for their
souls: beggars and prostitutes were carefully segregated.

With emphasis on the rights of the individual, the French
Revolution did not lead to improvement in poor relief but
to the reverse. Nor was the record of the Enlightenment
impressive in this area. Impatient with tradition and anti-
clerical, Enlightenment thinkers tended to be more fluent in
criticism of existing systems than practical in proposals for
better ones. The new breed of economists, the physiocrats,
were opposed to any interference with the laws of nature,
especially to any support that did not show a productive
return. The threat of social disorder did alarm the upper
class, however, and contributed to the revival in Britain of
Evangelical religion, which stressed elementary education
for the poor, reform of prisons, and abolition of the slave
trade and slavery. Meanwhile, the Holy Roman emperor
Joseph II had harnessed new funds for orphanages, hospitals, medical schools, and special institutions for the blind
and the insane. In 1785 the Vienna General Hospital had
2,000 beds. There was provision for deprived children of all
sorts. Graduated charges and free medical care for paupers
were among features of a policy that represented the utilitarian spirit at its most humane.

THE ORGANIZATION OF SOCIETY

The political history of Europe is inevitably the history of
privileged minorities. In states of the eastern and northern fringes, "the political nation"—comprising those

individuals who had some notion of loyalties beyond the parish and civil duties, if only at a local level, at the occasional diet, or in the army—hardly extended beyond the ranks of the gentry. Where they were numerous (a tenth of the population in Poland, for example), many would maintain themselves as clients of a magnate; even when theoretically independent, they would be likely to envisage the state in terms of sectional interest. The political life of England and Holland and the growing administration of France, Spain, and some German states opened doors to more sophisticated citizenship. Generally, however, political concerns were beyond the ken of peasants or ordinary townspeople for whom the state existed remotely, in the person of the prince, or directly, in that of the tax collector or billeting officer. It does not follow that it is futile to portray the people as a whole. First, however, it is necessary to identify certain characteristics of their world.

It was a Christian society which accepted, in and over the animist world where magic held many in thrall, the sovereignty of God and his laws. A priest might use folklore to convey the Christian message and expect allegiance so long as he endorsed paramount loyalties to family and parish. He might lose them if he objected too strongly to vendetta, charivari, and other forms of collective violence or simply to his parishioners' preference for tavern over church. Catholic or Protestant, he might preach against superstition, but he was as likely to denounce the witch as to curb her persecutors. He might see no end to his war against ignorance and sin; and he might falter in assurance of the love of God for suffering humanity. No more than any layperson was he immune to doubt and despair. But the evidence is unambiguous: the framework was hardly shaken. It was Christian doubt or Christian pessimism, all under the judgment of God. The priest in the confessional or the Protestant minister, Bible in hand, could look to that transcendent idea to support his vision of heaven's joys or hell's torments, of the infinite glory of God and the angels as portrayed by artists in the new Baroque style and of the machinations of the Devil and his minions.

The churches were the grandest expression of the community ideal, which shaped life at all levels and which can be seen in the Christian rites invariably used to enforce rules and cement fellowship. It also informed the guilds, professional and municipal corporations, and colleges that served the needs of craftsmen and tradesmen, inhabitants of cities, and scholars. The idea that society was composed of orders was given perhaps excessively precise form by the lawyer Charles Loyseau in his *Traité des Ordres* (1610), but it serves to stress the significance of precedence. It was assumed that society was hierarchical and that each order had divine sanction. Wherever a man found himself, at prayer or study, under arms or at work, there were collective rights and duties that had evolved as a strategy for survival. With them went the sense of belonging to a family of mutual obligations that had been a civilizing aspect of feudal society.

Feudalism, as a set of political arrangements, was dead by 1600. But aspects of feudal society survived, notably in the countryside. Various forms of personal service were owed by peasants to landowners and, in armies and courts, assumption of office and terms of service reflected the dealings of earlier times when power lay in the ownership of land. At the highest, providing cohesion in the intermediate phase between feudal and bureaucratic regimes, the patron-client relationship contained an idea of service that was nearer to medieval allegiance than to modern contract. Liveries might be out of use, but loyalty was owed to "my lord and master": a powerful man such as Richelieu could thus describe his service to a greater patron, Louis XIII, and would expect the same from his dependents. Envisaging such a society, the reader must dismiss the idea of natural rights, which was not current until the last decades of the 18th century. Rights accrued by virtue of belonging, in two ways: first, as the subject of a prince or equivalent authority—for example, magistrates of a free town or the bishop of an ecclesiastical principality; second, as the member of a community or corporation, in which one had rights depending on the rank into which one was born or on one's craft or profession. Whatever the formula by which such rights were expressed, it would be defended with tenacity as the means of ensuring the best possible life.

Christian, corporate (or communal), feudal: each label goes only some way to defining elusive mentalities in preindustrial society. The elements of organization that they represent look artificial unless the domestic basis is taken into account. The family was the lifeblood of all associations, giving purpose and identity to people who were rarely in crowds and knew nothing like the large, impersonal organization of modern times. To stress the family is not to sentimentalize it but to provide a key to understanding a near-vanished society. The intimacies of domestic life could not anesthetize against pain and hunger: life was not softened and death was a familiar visitor. Children were especially vulnerable but enjoyed no special status. Valued as an extra pair of hands or deplored as an extra mouth to feed, the child belonged to no privileged realm of play and protection from life's responsibilities. The family might be extended by numerous relations living nearby; in Mediterranean lands it was common for grandparents or brothers and sisters, married or single, to share a house or farm. Especially in more isolated communities, inbreeding added genetic hazards to the struggle for life. Everywhere the hold of the family, and of the father over the family, strengthened by laws of property and inheritance, curtained life's narrow windows from glimpses of a freer world. It affected marriage, since land, business, and dowry were customarily of more weight than the feelings of the bride and groom. But into dowries and ceremonies long saved for would go the display required to sustain the family name. Pride of family was one aspect of the craving for office. Providing status as well as security in a hierarchical society, it was significantly weaker in the countries, notably the United Provinces and England, where trading opportunities were greatest.

NOBLES AND GENTLEMEN

Between persistent poverty and the prevailing aristocratic spirit several connections can be made. The strong appeal of noble status and values was a force working generally against the pursuit of wealth and the investment that was to lead, precociously and exceptionally in Britain, to the Industrial Revolution. In France a nobleman could lose rank (*dérogeance*) by working, which inhibited him from engaging in any but a few specified enterprises. The typical relationship between landed gentleman and peasant producer was still feudal; whether represented by a range of rights and dues or by the more rigorous form of serfdom, it encouraged acceptance of the status quo in agriculture. Every state in Europe, except some Swiss cantons, recognized some form of nobility whose privileges were protected by law. Possession of land was a characteristic mark and aspiration of the elites.

The use of the two terms "nobleman" and "gentleman" indicates the difficulty of definition. The terms were loosely used to mark the essential distinction between members of an upper class and the rest. In France, above knights and esquires without distinctive title, ranged barons, viscounts, counts, and marquises, until the summit was reached with dukes and princes of the blood. In Britain, by contrast, peers of the realm—whether entitled duke, marquess, earl, or baron—numbered under 200 and enjoyed few special privileges beyond membership of the House of Lords. The gentry, however, with assured social position, knighthoods, armorial bearings, and estates, were the equivalent of Continental nobles. With the nobility, they owned more than three-quarters of the land: in contrast, in France by 1789 the nobility owned barely a third. In northern and eastern Europe, where the social structure was generally simpler than in the west, nobles—*dvoriane* in Russia, *szlachta* in Poland and Hungary—were numerous. In these countries, many of those technically noble were in reality of little importance and might even, like the "barefoot *szlachta*," have no land.

Such differences apart, there were rights and privileges that most Continental nobles possessed and values to which most subscribed. The right to wear a sword, to bear a crested coat of arms, to retain a special pew in church, to enjoy such precedence on formal occasions as rank prescribed, and to have if necessary a privileged form of trial would all seem to the noble inherent and natural. As landowner he enjoyed rights over peasants, not least as judge in his own court. In France, parts of Germany, Italy, and Spain, even if he did not own the land, he could as lord still benefit from feudal dues. He could hope for special favours from his sovereign or other patron in the form of a pension or office. There were vital exemptions, as from billeting soldiers and—most valuable—from taxation. The effectiveness of governments can be measured by the extent to which they breached this principle: in France, for example, in the 18th century by the *dixième* and *vingtième* taxes, effectively on income; belatedly, in Poland, where nobles paid no tax until the chimney tax of 1775. Generally they could expect favourable treatment: special schools, privileges at university, preferment in the church, commissions in the army. They could assume that a sovereign, while encroaching on their rights, would yet share their values. Richelieu's policy exemplifies such ambivalence. A noble himself, Richelieu sought to promote the interests of his class while directing it toward royal service and clipping the wings of the over-powerful. Frederick II the Great of Prussia was not concerned about faction. Since "most commoners think meanly," he believed that nobles were best suited to serve in the government and the army. Such admiration for noble virtues did not usually extend to the political role. The decline of Continental diets, with the growth of bureaucracies, largely recruited from commoners, did not mean, however, even in the west, that nobility was in retreat before the rise of the bourgeoisie. Through social preeminence, nobles maintained—and in the 18th century even tightened—their hold on the commanding heights in church and state.

Within all countries there was a distinction between higher and lower levels within the caste: in some, not only between those who were titled and the rest but, as in Spain and France, between *titulos* and grandees, a small group upon which royal blood or the achievement of some ancestor conferred privileges of a self-perpetuating kind. "The grandeeship of the counts of Lemos was made by God and time," observed the head of the family to the new Bourbon king Philip V. No less pretentious were the Condés or the Montmorencys of France. There was a tendency everywhere to the aggrandizement of estates through arranged marriage, a sovereign's favour, or the opportunities provided by war, as in Bohemia after the suppression of the revolt of 1618 or in England with the rise of the Whig families of Russell and Cavendish. In Britain, the principle of primogeniture ensured succession to the eldest son (promoting social mobility as younger sons made their way in professions or trades). Peter I the Great of Russia legislated for the entail (1714), but without success: it was abandoned by Anna (1731) in favour of the traditional law of inheritance. However, *mayorazgo* in Castile and *fideicommissum* in parts of Italy kept vast estates together. Where the colonization of new lands was not restrained by central government, families like the Radziwiłłs and Wiśniowieckis of Poland acquired huge estates. The *szlachta* of Hungary also cherished privileges as descendants of warriors and liberators. There, Prince Miklós Esterházy, patron of a private orchestra and of Joseph Haydn, excelled all by the end of the 17th century with his annual revenue of 700,000 florins. In Russia, where wealth was measured in serfs, Prince Cherkanski was reckoned in 1690 to have 9,000 peasant households.

Status increasingly signified economic circumstances. In France, where subtle nuances escaped the outsider, one trend is revealing. The old distinction between "sword" and "gown" lost much importance. Age of title came to mean more for antiquarians and purists than for men of fashion who would not scorn a mésalliance if it "manured the land." Most daughters of 18th-century tax farmers married the sons of nobles. The class was open to new creations, usually through purchase of an office conferring nobility. When, in a regulation of 1760, the year 1400 was made a test of antiquity, fewer than 1,000 families were eligible. The tendency was toward the formation of a plutocracy. Nobles came to dominate the church and the army, even to penetrate government, from which it had been the policy of the early Bourbons to exclude them. The noble order numbered about 120,000 families by 1789. By then the nobles, particularly those of the country who seldom came to court, had brought their rearguard action to a climax to preserve their privileges—for example, by Ségur's ordinance of 1781, reserving army commissions to nobles of at least four generations. This "feudal reaction" contributed to the problems of government in the years before the Revolution. In Russia, at the height of the conservative reaction that had already secured the abolition (1762) of the service obligation imposed by Peter I, Catherine II the Great was forced to abandon liberal reforms. The Pugachov rising (1773–74) alerted landowners to the dangers of serfdom, but it was reckoned that three-fifths of all landowners owned fewer than 20 serfs. The census of 1687 showed that there were half a million nobles in Spain. But *hidalguia* might mean little more than a Spaniard's estimation of himself. Without a substantial *señorio* (estate), the hidalgo was insignificant.

When "living nobly" meant not working and hidalgos or *szlachta* attached themselves to a great house for a coat and a loaf, faction became more dangerous and aristocratic interests more resistant to change. It took courage for a sovereign to tackle the entrenched power of nobility in diets, as did the Habsburg queen Maria Theresa (1740–80) in her Austrian and Bohemian lands. Nowhere in Europe did nobles take themselves more seriously, but they were the readier to accept curtailment of their political rights because they enjoyed a healthy economic position. Vienna's cosmopolitan culture and Baroque palaces were evidence of not only the success of the regime in drawing nobles to the capital but also the rise in manorial rents. Nobles played a decorative role in the most ceremonious court in 18th-century Europe. Charles VI (1711–40) had provided 40,000 posts for noble clients. Maria Theresa, concerned about expense, reduced the number of chamberlains to 1,500. It was left to her son Joseph II to attack noble privileges at every point, right up to the abolition of serfdom. There was a correlation between the advance of government and the curtailment of noble privilege. Inevitably it was an uneven process, depending much on the resolution of a ruler. In Sweden it was to the poor gentlemen, a high proportion of its 10,000 nobles, that Charles XI had appealed in his successful promotion of absolutist reforms in the 1680s. After 1718 the same conservative force militated against royal government. The aristocratic reaction of the age of liberty saw the reassertion of the traditional principle that the nobility were the guardians of the country's liberties. So the Swedish upper class arrived at the position of their British counterparts and obtained that power, not divorced from responsibility, which was envied and extolled by the French thinkers who regretted its absence from France and sought consolation in the works of Montesquieu. A central idea of his *L'Esprit des lois* (1748; *The Spirit of Laws*) was that noble privilege was the surest guarantee of the laws against despotism. That could not be said of Prussia, although a Junker's privilege was wedded to a subject's duty. In exchange for the loss of political rights, Junkers had been confirmed in their social and fiscal privileges: with the full rigour of serfdom (*Leibeigenschaft*) and rights of jurisdiction over tenants went a secure hold over local government. Under the pressure of war and following his own taste for aristocratic manners, Frederick II taught them to regard the army or civil service as a career. But Frederick disappointed the intellectuals who expected him to protect the peasantry. The nobles meanwhile acquired a pride in militarism that was to be potent in the creation of the 19th-century German state. The class became more numerous but remained relatively poor: Junkers often had to sell land to supplement meagre pay. Frederick's working nobility sealed the achievements of his capable predecessors. The price paid indicates the difficulties inherent in any attempt to reconcile the interests of the dominant class to the needs of society.

Nobility also had a civilizing role. Europe would be immeasurably poorer without the music, literature, and architecture of the age of aristocracy. The virtues of Classical taste were to some extent those of aristocracy: splendour restrained by formal rules and love of beauty uninhibited by utilitarian considerations. There was much that was absurd in the pretensions of some patrons; illusions of grandeur are rarely the best basis for the conceiving of great art. The importance of bourgeois patronage should not be overlooked, otherwise no account would be taken of Holland's golden age. Where taste was unaffected by the need for display (as could not be said of Louis XIV's Versailles) or where a wise patron put his trust in the reputedly best architect, art could triumph. Civilizing trends were prominent, as in England, where there was a free intellectual life. New money, as lavished by the duke of Chandos, builder of the great house of Canons and patron of the composer George Frideric Handel, could be fruitful. Also important was the fusion of aristocratic style with ecclesiastical patronage, as could occur where noblemen enjoyed the best preferment and abbots lived like nobles: the glories of the German Baroque at Melk, Ottobeuren, and Vierzehnheiligen speak as much of aristocracy as of the Christian Gospel.

In contrast with Sweden, where, in the 18th century, talent was recognized and the scientists Carolus Linnaeus and Emanuel Swedenborg were ennobled, or France, where the plutocracy encountered the Enlightenment without discomfort, the most sterile ground for aristocratic culture was to be found where there was an enforced isolation, as in Spain or Europe's poor marches and remotest western shores. Visitors to Spain were startled by the ignorance of the men and the passivity of the women. Life in Poland, Hungary, and Ireland resolved itself for many of the gentry into a simple round of hunting and carousing. The urban aspect of noble culture needs stress, which is not surprising when its Classical inspiration is recalled.

Even in England, where educated men favoured country life and did not despise the country town, society would have been poorer without the intense activity of London. All the greater was the importance of the capital cities—Warsaw, St. Petersburg, Budapest, and Dublin—in countries that might not otherwise have generated fine art or architecture.

The aristocratic spirit transcended frontiers. For the nobleman Europe was the homeland. Italian plasterers and painters, German musicians, and French cabinetmakers traveled for high commissions. There were variations reflecting local traditions: the Baroque style was interpreted distinctively in Austria, Italy, Spain, and France. But high style reveals certain underlying principles and convictions. The same is true of the intellectual life of Europe, reflecting as it did two main sources, French and English. It was especially to France that the two most powerful rulers of eastern Europe, Frederick II of Prussia and Catherine II of Russia, looked for mentors in thought and style. The French language, deliberately purified from the time of Richelieu and the foundation of the French Academy, was well adapted to the clear expression of ideas. The salons stimulated the discussion of ideas and engendered a distinctive style. Feminine insights there contributed to a rational culture that was also responsive to the claims of sensibility.

THE BOURGEOISIE

The European bourgeoisie presents faces so different that common traits can be discerned only at the simplest level: the possession of property with the desire and means to increase it, emancipation from past precepts about investment, a readiness to work for a living, and a sense of being superior to town workers or peasants. With their social values—sobriety, discretion, and economy—went a tendency to imitate the style of their social superiors. In France, the expectations of the bourgeoisie were roused by education and relative affluence to the point at which they could be a revolutionary force once the breakdown of royal government and its recourse to a representative assembly had given them the voice they had lacked. Everywhere the Enlightenment was creating a tendency to be critical of established institutions (notably, in Roman Catholic countries, the church), together with a hunger for knowledge as a tool of progress.

Such dynamic characteristics, conducive to social mobility, should not obscure the essential feature of bourgeois life: conservativism within a corporate frame. In 1600, a town of more than 100,000 would have been thought enormous: only London, Paris, Naples, Seville, Venice, Rome, and Constantinople came into that class. Half in Asia but enmeshed in the European economic system, Constantinople was unique: it was a megalopolis, a gigantic consumer of the produce of subject lands. London's growth was more significant for the future: it was a seaport and capital, but with a solid base in manufacturing, trade, and finance. Like Naples, it was a magnet for the unemployed and restless. In 1700 there were only 48 towns in Europe with a population of more than 40,000; all were regarded as important places. Even a smaller city might have influence in the country, offering a range of services and amenities; such was Amiens, with 30,000 inhabitants and 36 guilds, including bleachers, dyers, and finishers of the cloth that was woven in nearby villages but sent far afield. Most towns had fewer than 10,000 inhabitants, and a fair number only about 1,000; most towns remained static or declined. Some grew, however: between 1600 and 1750 the proportion of the population living in towns of

Bourgeoisie

The social order that is dominated by the so-called middle class is known as the bourgeoisie. In popular speech, the term connotes philistinism, materialism, and a striving concern for "respectability," all of which were famously ridiculed by French playwright Molière (1622–73) and criticized by avant-garde playwrights since Henrik Ibsen (1828–1906). The term *bourgeois* arose in medieval France, where it denoted an inhabitant of a walled town. Its overtones became important in the 18th century, when the middle class of professionals, manufacturers, and their literary and political allies began to demand an influence in politics consistent with their economic status. Karl Marx (1818–83) was one of many thinkers who treated the French Revolution as a revolution of the bourgeois.

more than 20,000 doubled from 4 to 8 percent, representing about half the total urban population.

A universal phenomenon was the growth of capital cities, which benefited from the expansion of government, particularly if, as was usual, the court was within the city. Growth could acquire its own momentum, irrespective of the condition of the country: besides clients and servants of all kinds, artisans, shopkeepers, and other providers of services swelled the ranks. Warsaw's size doubled during Poland's century of distress to stand at 120,000 by 1772. St. Petersburg, in 1700 a swamp, acquired 218,000 inhabitants by 1800. Berlin, the simple electoral capital of some 6,000 inhabitants in 1648, rose with the success of the Hohenzollerns to a population of 150,000 by 1786. By then the population of Vienna—home of the imperial court, a growing professional class, a renowned university and other schools, and hospitals—had reached 220,000. The population of Turin, capital of relatively small Savoy, also doubled in the 18th century.

Rome did not suffer too obviously from the retreat of the popes from a leading political role, but the Holy City (140,000 inhabitants in 1700) was top-heavy, with little in the way of manufacturing. All these cities owed their growth to their strategic place in the government rather than to their economic importance.

Other cities grew around specialized industries or from opportunities for a wider trade than was possible where markets were limited by the range of horse and mule. Growth was likely to be slow where, as in Lyon, Rouen, and Dresden, production continued to be along traditional lines or, in ports such as Danzig, Königsberg, or Hamburg, where trading patterns remained essentially the same. Enterprise, by contrast, brought remarkable growth in Britain, where Manchester and Birmingham both moved up from modest beginnings to the 100,000-population mark during the 18th century. Atlantic ports thrived during the same period with the increase in colonial trade: into this category fall Bordeaux, Nantes, Bristol, Liverpool, and Glasgow. Marseille recovered quickly from the plague of 1720 and grew on the grain import trade; more typical of Mediterranean cities were stagnant Genoa, Venice, and Palermo, where Austrian policy in the 18th century, favouring Milan, was an adverse factor.

A typical urban experience, where there was no special factor at work, was therefore one of stability. The burgher of 1600 would have felt at home in the town of his descendant five generations later. There might have been calamities along the way: at worst, siege or assault, plague, a particularly serious recession, or a fire, such as destroyed Rennes in 1720. Some building or refacing of houses would have occurred, mainly within the walls. In more fortunate cities, where there was continuing economic stability or strong corporate identity—as in the siege victims La Rochelle (1628) or Magdeburg (1631)—recovery even from the worst of war experiences could be rapid. The professions, notably the church and law, were tough, having large interests in the town and in the property in and around it. Guild discipline, inhibiting in fair years, was a strength in foul ones. Not all towns were so resilient, however. Some Polish towns never recovered from the effects of the Great Northern War; others throughout northern and eastern Europe were victims of the rise of the self-sufficient estate, which supplied needs such as brewing that the town had previously offered. Some Italian and Spanish towns, such as Cremona, Toledo, and Burgos, were affected by the decline of manufacturing and the shift of trade to the Atlantic economies.

It was possible for a town that had a special importance in the sphere of church or law (Angers, Salzburg, or Trier, for example) to enjoy a quiet prosperity, but there was a special kind of deadness about towns that had no other raison d'être than to be host to numerous clergy. Valladolid contained 53 religious houses "made up principally of consumers" according to a report of 1683. Most numerous were the quiet places that had never grown from their basic function of providing a market. England's archaic electoral system provided graphic evidence of such decay, leaving its residue of "rotten boroughs."

Between these extremes lay the mass of towns of middling size, each supervised by a mayor and corporation, dignified by one large church and probably several others serving ward or parish (and, if Catholic, by a religious house of some kind), and including a law court, guildhall, school, and, of course, market. With its bourgeois crust of clerics, lawyers, officials, merchants, and shopkeepers and master craftsmen catering for special needs—fine fabrics, clothing, hats, wigs, gloves, eyeglasses, engravings if not paintings, china, silver, glassware, locks, and clocks—the city was a world apart from the peasant. The contrast was emphasized by the walls, the gates that closed at night, the cobbles or setts of the roads, the different speech and intonation, the well-fed look of some citizens, and above all the fine houses, suggesting as much an ordered way of life as the wealth that supported it. The differences were blurred, however, by the pursuits of the urban landowners; by ubiquitous animals, whether bound for market or belonging to the citizens; by the familiar poverty and filth of the streets and the reek of the tannery and the shambles.

It is easier to re-create the physical frame than the mentalities of townspeople. Letters, journals, government reports and statistics, wills, and contracts reveal salient features. The preference for safe kinds of investment could be exploited by governments for revenue, as notably by the French: in 1661 Colbert found that, of 46,000 offices of justice and finance, 40,000 were unnecessary. There was an inclination to buy land for status and security. Around cities like Dijon, most of the surrounding land was owned by the bourgeois or the recently ennobled. Custom and ceremony were informed by a keen sense of hierarchy, as in minutely ordered processions. The instinct to regulate was stiffened by the need to restrain servants and journeymen and to ensure that apprentices waited for the reward of their training. Religion maintained its hold more firmly in the smaller towns, while the law was respected as the mainstay of social order and the road to office in courts or administration even where, as in Italy, it was palpably corruptible. There were certain communal dreads, military requisitioning and billeting high among them. There was generally a resolve to ward off beggars, to maintain grain stores, to close the gates to the famished when crops failed, and to enforce quarantine.

Within towns, popular forms of government were abandoned as power was monopolized by groups of wealthy men. This process can be studied in the Dutch

towns in the years after 1648 when regents gained control. Everywhere elites were composed of those who had
no business role. Among other labels for this period, when
a profession seemed to be more desirable than trade, "a
time of lawyers" might be appropriate. Trained to contend,
responsive to new ideas, at least dipping into the waters of
the Enlightenment, those lawyers who were cheated, by
sheer numbers, of the opportunity to rise might become
a dissident element, especially in countries where political avenues were blocked and the economy was growing
too slowly to sustain them. Sometimes the state moved in
to control municipal affairs, as in France where intendants
were given wide powers toward the end of Louis XIV's reign.
In Spain, towns came into the hands of local magnates.

A more serious threat to the old urban regime lay in
another area where discontents bred radicalism: the guilds.
Not until the French Revolution and the radical actions
of Joseph II of Austria were guilds anywhere abolished.
They had long displayed a tendency to oligarchic control
by hereditary masters. They became more restrictive in
the face of competition and growing numbers of would-be
members and so drove industries, particularly those
suited to dispersed production, back to the countryside.
For this reason, such cities as Leiden, Rouen, Cologne,
and Nürnberg actually lost population in the 18th century.
To compensate for falling production, masters tended to
put pressure on the relatively unskilled level, where there
were always more workers than work. Journeymen's associations sought to improve their situation, sometimes
through strikes. The building trade was notorious for its
secret societies. The decline of the guilds was only one
symptom of the rise in population. Another was the rise
in urban poverty, as pressure on resources led to price
increases that outstripped wages. In late 18th-century
Berlin, which was solidly based on bureaucracy, garrison,

and numerous crafts, a third of the population still lacked regular work. The plight of the poor was emphasized by the affluence of increasing numbers of fellow citizens. However class conflict is interpreted, it is clear that its basic elements were by that time present and active.

THE PEASANTRY

In 1700 only 15 percent of Europe's population lived in towns, but that figure concealed wide variations: at the two extremes by 1800 were Britain with 40 percent and Russia with 4 percent. Most Europeans were peasants, dependent on agriculture. The majority of them lived in nucleated settlements and within recognized boundaries, those of parish or manor, but some, in the way characteristic of the hill farmer, lived in single farms or hamlets. The type of settlement reflected its origins: pioneers who had cleared forests or drained swamps, Germans who had pressed eastward into Slav lands, Russians who had replaced conquered Mongols, Spaniards who had expelled the Moors. Each brought distinctive characteristics. Discounting the nomad fringe, there remains a fundamental difference between serfs and those who had more freedom, whether as owners or tenants paying some form of rent but both liable to seigneurial dues. There were about one million serfs in eastern France and some free peasants in Russia, so the pattern is untidy; but broadly it represents the difference between eastern and western Europe.

The Russian was less attached to a particular site than his western counterparts living in more densely populated countries and had to be held down by a government determined to secure taxes and soldiers. The imposition of serfdom was outlined in the Ulozhenie, the legal code of 1649, which included *barschina* (forced labour). One consequence was the decline of the mir, the village community, with its fellowship and practical services; another was the tightening of the ties of mutual interest that bound tsar and landowner. Poles, Germans (mainly those of the east and north), Bohemians, and Hungarians were subject to a serfdom less extreme only in that they were treated as part of the estate and could not be sold separately; the Russian serf, who could, was more akin to a slave. Russian state peasants, an increasingly numerous class in the 18th century, were not necessarily secure; they were sent out to farm new lands. Catherine the Great transferred 800,000 serfs to private ownership. The serf could not marry, move, or take up a trade without his lord's leave. He owed labour (*robot*) in the Habsburg lands for at least three days a week and dues that could amount to 20 percent of his produce. The Thirty Years' War hastened the process of subjection, already fed by the west's demand for grain; peasants returning to ruined homesteads found that their rights had vanished. The process was resisted by some rulers, notably those of Saxony and Brunswick: independent peasants were a source of revenue. Denmark saw an increase in German-style serfdom in the 18th century, but most Swedish peasants were free—their enemies were climate and hunger, rather than the landowner. Uniquely, they had representation in their own Estate in the Riksdag (diet).

Through much of Germany, France, Italy, Spain, and Portugal there was some form of rent or sharecropping. Feudalism survived in varying degrees of rigour, with an array of dues and services representing seigneurial rights. It was a regime that about half of Europe's inhabitants had known since the Middle Ages. In England, all but a few insignificant forms had gone, though feudal spirit lingered in deference to the squire. Enclosures were reducing the yeoman to the condition of a tenant farmer or, for most, a dependent, landless labourer. Although alodial tenures (absolute ownership) ensured freedom from dues in some southern provinces, France provides the best model for understanding the relationship of lord and peasant. The seigneur was generally, but not invariably, noble: a seigneury could be bought by a commoner. It had two parts. The *domaine* was the house with its grounds: there were usually a church and a mill, but not necessarily fields and woods, for those might have been sold. The *censives*, lands subject to the seigneur, still owed dues even if no longer owned by him. The *cens*, paid annually, was significant because it represented the obligations of the peasant: free to buy and sell land, he still endured burdens that varied from the trivial or merely vexatious to those detrimental to good husbandry. They were likely to include *banalités*, monopoly rights over the mill, wine press, or oven; *saisine* and *lods et ventes*, respectively a levy on the assets of a *censitaire* on death and a purchase tax on property sold; *champart*, a seigneurial tithe, payable in kind; monopolies of hunting, shooting, river use, and pigeon rearing; the privilege of the first harvest, for example, *droit de banvin*, by which the seigneur could gather his grapes and sell his wine first; and the corvées, obligatory labour services. Seigneurial rule had benevolent aspects, and justice in the seigneurial court could be even-handed; seigneurs could be protectors of the community against the state's taxes and troops. But the regime was damaging, as much to the practice of farming as to the life of the peasants, who were harassed and schooled in resistance and concealment. To identify an 18th-century feudal reaction—as some historians have called the tendency to apply business principles to the management of dues—is not to obscure the fact that for many seigneurs the system was becoming unprofitable. By 1789, in most provinces there was little hesitation: the National Assembly abolished feudal dues by decree at one sitting because the peasants had already taken the law into their own hands. Some rights were won back, but there could be no wholesale restoration.

Besides priest or minister, the principal authority in most peasants' lives was that of the lord. The collective will of the community also counted for much, as in arrangements for plowing, sowing, and reaping, and even in some places the allocation of land. The range of the peasant's world was that of a day's travel on foot or, more likely, by donkey, mule, or pony. He would have little sense of a community larger than he could see or visit. His struggle against nature or the demands of his superiors was waged in countless little pockets. When peasants came together in insurgent bands, as in Valencia in 1693, there was likely to be some agitation or leadership from outside the peasant community—in that case from José Navarro, a surgeon. There needed to be some exceptional provocation, like the new tax that roused Brittany in 1675. After the revolt had been suppressed, the *parlement* of Rennes was exiled to a smaller town for 14 years: clearly government understood the danger of bourgeois complicity. Rumour was always potent, especially when tinged with fantasy, as in Stenka Razin's rising in southern Russia, which evolved between 1667 and 1671 from banditry into a vast protest against serfdom. Generally, cooperation between villages was less common than feuding, the product of centuries of uneasy proximity and conflict over disputed lands.

The peasant's life was conditioned by mundane factors: soil, water supplies, communications, and above all the site itself in relation to river, sea, frontier, or strategic route. The community could be virtually self-sufficient. Its environment was formed by what could be bred, fed, sown, gathered, and worked within the bounds of the parish. Fields and beasts provided food and clothing; wood came from the fringe of wasteland. Except in districts where stone was available and easy to work, houses were usually made of wood or a cob of clay and straw. Intended to provide shelter from the elements, they can be envisaged as a refinement of the barn, with certain amenities for their human occupants: hearth, table, and benches with mats and rushes strewn on a floor of beaten earth or rough stone. Generally there would be a single story, with a raised space for beds and an attic for grain. For his own warmth and their security the peasant slept close to his animals, under the same roof. Cooking required an iron pot, sometimes the only utensil named in peasant inventories. Meals were eaten off wood or earthenware. Fuel was normally wood, which was becoming scarce in some intensively cultivated parts of northern Europe, particularly Holland, where much of the land was reclaimed from sea or marsh. Peat and dried dung also were used, but rarely coal. Corn was ground at the village mill, a place of potential conflict: only one man had the necessary expertise, and his clients were poorly placed to bargain. Women and girls spun and wove for the itinerant merchants who supplied the wool or simply for the household, for breeches, shirts, tunics, smocks, and gowns. Clothes served elemental needs: they were usually thick for protection against damp and cold and loose-fitting for ease of movement. Shoes were likely to be wooden clogs, as leather was needed for harnesses. Farm implements—plows (except for the share), carts, harrows, and many of the craftsman's tools—were made of wood, seasoned, split or rough-hewn. Few possessed saws; in Russia they were unknown before 1700. Iron was little used and was likely to be of poor quality. Though it might be less true of eastern Europe where, as in Bohemia, villages tended to be smaller, the community would usually have craftsmen—a smith or a carpenter, for example—to satisfy most needs. More intricate skills were provided by traveling tinkers.

The isolated villager might hear of the outside world from such men. Those living around the main routes would fare better and gather news, at least indirectly, from merchants, students, pilgrims, and government officials or, less reputably, from beggars, gypsies, or deserters (a numerous class in most states). He might buy broadsheets, almanacs, and romances, produced by enterprising printers at centres such as Troyes, to be hawked around wherever there were a few who could read. So were kept alive what became a later generation's fairy tales, along with the magic and astrology that they were not reluctant to believe. Inn and church provided the setting for business, gossip, and rumour. Official reports and requirements were posted and village affairs were conducted in the church. The innkeeper might benefit from the cash of wayfarers but like others who provided a service, he relied chiefly on the produce of his own land. Thus the rural economy consisted of innumerable self-sufficient units incapable of generating adequate demand for the development of large-scale manufactures. Each cluster of communities was isolated within its own market economy, proud, and suspicious of outsiders. Even where circumstances fostered liberty, peasants were pitifully inadequate in finding original solutions to age-old problems but were well-versed in strategies of survival, for they could draw on stores of empirical wisdom. They feared change just as they feared the night for its unknown terrors. Their customs and attitudes were those of people who lived on the brink: more babies might be born but there would be no increase in the food supply.

In the subsistence economy there was much payment and exchange in kind; money was hoarded for the occasional purchase, to the frustration of tax collectors and the detriment of economic growth. Demand was limited by the slow or nonexistent improvement in methods of farming. There was no lack of variety in the agricultural landscape. Between the temporary cultivation of parts of Russia and Scandinavia, where slash-and-burn was encouraged by the extent of forest land, and the rotation of cereal and fodder crops of Flanders and eastern England, 11 different methods of tillage have been identified. Most common was some version of the three-course rotation that Arthur Young denounced when he traveled in France in 1788. He observed the subdivision and wide dispersal of holdings that provided a further obstacle to the diversification of crops and selective breeding. The loss of land by enclosure pauperized many English labourers. But the development in lowland England of the enclosed, compact economic unit—the central feature of the agrarian revolution—enabled large landowners to prosper and invest and small farmers to survive. They were not trapped, like many Continental peasants, between the need to cultivate more land and the declining yields of their crops, which followed from the loss of pasture and of fertilizing manure. Without capital accumulation and with persisting low demand for goods, economic growth was inhibited. The workforce was therefore tied to agriculture in numbers that depressed wage rates, discouraged innovation, and tempted landowners to compensate by some form of exploitation of labour, rights, and dues. Eighteenth-century reformers condemned serfdom and other forms of feudalism, but they were as much the consequence as the cause of the agricultural malaise.

THE ECONOMIC ENVIRONMENT

Every country had challenges to overcome before its resources could be developed. The possession of a coastline with safe harbours or of a navigable river was an important asset and, as by Brandenburg and Russia, keenly fought for; so were large mineral deposits, forests, and fertile soil. But communications were primitive and transport slow and costly even in favoured lands. Napoleon moved at the same speed as Julius Caesar. By horse, coach, or ship, it was reckoned that 24 hours was necessary to travel 60 miles (96.6 km). In one area, however, innovation had proceeded at such a pace as to justify terms such as "intellectual" or "scientific" revolution; yet there remained a yawning gap between developments in theoretical science and technology. In the age of Newton the frontiers of science were shifting fast, and there was widespread interest in experiment and demonstration, but one effect was to complete the separation of a distinctive intellectual elite: the more advanced the ideas, the more difficult their transmission and application. There was a movement of thought rather than a scientific movement, a culture of inquiry rather than of enterprise. Only in the long term was the one to lead to the other, through the growing belief that material progress was possible. Meanwhile, advances were piecemeal, usually the work of individuals, often having no connection with business. Missing was not only that association of interests that characterizes industrial society but also the educational ground: schools and universities were wedded to traditional courses. Typical inventors of the early industrial age were untutored craftsmen, such as Richard Arkwright, James Watt, or John Wilkinson. Between advances in technology there could be long delays.

As those names suggest, Britain was the country that experienced the breakthrough to higher levels of production. The description "Industrial Revolution" is misleading if applied to the economy as a whole, but innovations in techniques and organization led to such growth in iron, woolens, and, above all, cotton textiles in the

second half of the 18th century that Britain established
a significant lead. It was sustained by massive investment and by the wars following the French Revolution,
which shut the Continent off from developments that in
Britain were stimulated by war. Factors involved in the
unique experience of a country that contained only 1 in
20 of Europe's inhabitants expose certain contrasting
features of the European economy. The accumulation
of capital had been assisted by agricultural improvement, the acquisition of colonies, the operation of
chartered companies (notably the East India Company),
trade-oriented policies of governments (notably that of
William Pitt during the Seven Years' War), and the development of colonial markets. There existed a relatively
advanced financial system, based on the successful Bank
of England (founded 1694), and interest rates were consistently lower than those of European rivals. This was
particularly important in the financing of road and canal
building, where large private investment was needed
before profit was realized. Further advantages included
plentiful coal and iron ore and swift-flowing streams in
the hilly northwest where the moist climate was suited
to cotton spinning. The labour force was supplemented
by Irish immigrants. A society that cherished traditional
political and legal institutions also exhibited a free and
tolerant spirit, tending to value fortune as much as birth.
Comparison with Britain's chief rival in the successive
wars of 1740–48, 1756–63, and 1778–83 is strengthened
by the consequences of those wars: for France the slide
toward bankruptcy, for Britain a larger debt that could
still be funded without difficulty.

Yet the French enjoyed an eightfold growth in colonial
trade between 1714 and 1789, considerably larger than that
of the British. The Dutch still had the financial strength,

colonies, trading connections, and at least some of the entrepreneurial spirit that had characterized them in the 17th century. Enlightened statesmen such as the marquês de Pombal in Portugal, Charles III of Spain, and Joseph II of Austria backed measures designed to promote agriculture and manufacturing. The question of why other countries lagged behind Britain leads to consideration of material and physical conditions, collective attitudes, and government policies. It should not distort the picture of Europe as a whole or obscure the changes that affected the demand for goods and the ability of manufacturers and traders to respond.

The mercantilist theory—which still appealed to a statesman like Frederick the Great of Prussia, as it had to his great-grandfather—was grounded on the assumption that markets were limited: to increase trade, new markets had to be found. Mobility within society and increased spending by common folk, who were not expected to live luxuriously, were treated as symptoms of disorder. Mercantilists were concerned lest the state be stripped of its treasure and proper distinctions of status be undermined. The moral context is important: mercantilism belongs to the world of the city-state, the guilds, and the church; its ethical teaching is anchored in the medieval situation. By 1600 the doctrine that usury was sinful was already weakened beyond recovery by evasion and example. Needy princes borrowed, but prejudice against banks lingered, reinforced by periodic demonstrations of their fallibility, as in the failure of John Law's Banque Générale in Paris in 1720. Productive activity was not necessarily assumed to be a good thing. Yet it is possible, throughout the period, to identify dynamic features characteristic of capitalism in its developed, industrial phase.

EARLY CAPITALISM

Two broad trends can be discerned. The shift from the Mediterranean and its hinterlands to the Atlantic seaboard continued, although there was still vigorous entrepreneurial activity in certain Mediterranean regions; Venice stood still, but Marseille and Barcelona prospered. More striking was the growing gap between the economic systems of the east, where capital remained largely locked up in the large estates, and the west, where conditions were more favourable to enterprise. With more widespread adoption of utilitarian criteria for management went a sterner view of the obligation of workers. Respect for the clock, with regular hours and the reduction of holidays for saints' days (already achieved in Protestant countries), was preparing the way psychologically for the discipline of the factory and mill. Handsome streets and squares of merchants' houses witnessed to the prosperity of Atlantic ports such as Bordeaux, Nantes, and Bristol, which benefited from the reorientation of trade. Above all, Amsterdam and London reflected the mutually beneficial activity of trade and services. From shipbuilding, so demanding in skills and raw materials, a network of suppliers reached back to forests, fields, and forges, where timber, iron, canvas, and rope were first worked. Chandlering, insurance, brokerage, and credit-trading facilitated international dealing and amassing of capital. Fairs had long counteracted the isolation of regional economies: Lyon on the Rhône, Hamburg on the Elbe, and Danzig on the Vistula had become centres of exchange, where sales were facilitated by price lists, auctions, and specialization in certain commodities. Retailing acquired a modern look with shops catering to those who could afford coffee from Brazil or tobacco from Virginia; unlike earlier retailing, the goods offered for sale were not the products of work carried out on the premises. The dissemination of news was another strand in the pattern. By 1753 the sale of newspapers exceeded seven million: the emphasis was on news, not opinion, and price lists were carried with the news that affected them. Seamen were assisted by the dredging of harbours and improved docks and by more accurate navigational instruments and charts. In 1600 there were 18 lighthouses on or off the shores of Europe; in 1750 there were 82. The state also improved roads and made them safe for travelers; by 1789 France had 7,500 miles (12,000 km) of fine roads, built largely by forced labour. By 1660 nearly every Dutch city was linked by canals. Following their example, Elector Frederick William in Brandenburg and Peter the Great in Russia linked rivers to facilitate trade. In France Colbert's plan for the Languedoc canal (completed 1682) involved private as well as state capital. England's canal builders, notably the duke of Bridgewater, had to find their own resources: consequently, capital was applied to the best effect to serve mines and factories. The general survival of tolls and the resistance of interested parties to their removal imposed constraints on most governments. The abolition of internal customs was therefore a priority for enlightened reformers such as Anne-Robert-Jacques Turgot in France and Joseph II in Austria. Germany's many princes had taken advantage of weak imperial authority to impose the tolls, which produced revenue at the cost of long-distance trade. Numerous external tariffs remained an obstacle to the growth of trade. Radical action, however, could be dangerous. Turgot's attempt to liberate the grain trade in France led to shortages, price rises, and his own downfall. The free trade treaty of 1786 of the French foreign minister, the comte de Vergennes, also had unfortunate consequences: France was flooded by cheap English textiles, peasant weavers were distressed, and the ground was prepared for the popular risings of 1789.

One important development was the adoption in western Europe of the existing Italian practice of using bills of exchange as negotiable instruments; it was legalized in Holland in 1651 and in England in 1704. Bankers who bought bills, at a discount to cover risk, thereby released credit that would otherwise have been immobilized. The other aspect of the financial revolution was the growth of banking facilities. In 1660 there had been little advance in a century, since princes and magnates, after raising money too easily, had reneged on debts and damaged the fragile system. Great houses, such as the Fuggers, had been ruined. The high interest rates demanded by survivors contributed to the recession of the 17th century. There were some municipal institutions, such as the Bank of Hamburg and the great Bank of Amsterdam, which played a crucial part in Dutch economic growth by bringing order to the currency and facilitating transfers. They provided the model for the Bank of England, which was founded in 1694 as a private company and was soon to have a relationship of mutual dependence with the state. The first state bank was that founded in Sweden in 1656; to provide a substitute for Sweden's copper currency, it issued the first bank notes. Overproduced and not properly secured, they soon lost value. Law's ambitious scheme for a royal bank in France foundered in 1720 because it was linked to his Louisiana company and its inflated prospects. After its failure tax farmers resumed their hold over state finance, and as a result interest rates remained higher than those of Britain because there was no secure central agency of investment. Law's opponents were shortsighted: in Britain, where a central bank was successful, a large expansion of private banking also took place.

Meanwhile silver, everywhere the basic unit of value, remained in short supply. One-sided trade with the east meant a continuous drain. Insufficient silver was mined; declining imports from the New World did not affect only Spain. Governments tried to prevent the clipping of coins and so revalued. The deficiency remained, providing evidence for mercantilist policies. Negotiable paper in one form or other went some way to meet the shortage of specie. Stock exchanges, commercial in their original function, dealt increasingly in government stocks. Joint-stock companies became a common device for attracting money and spreading risk. By the mid-18th century the operations of commerce, manufacturing, and public finance were linked in one general system; a military defeat or economic setback affecting credit in one area might undermine confidence throughout the entire investing community.

THE OLD INDUSTRIAL ORDER

Operations of high finance represented the future of capitalist Europe. The economy as a whole was still closer in most respects to the Middle Ages. Midland and northern England, a belt along the Urals, Catalonia, the Po valley, and Flanders were scenes of exceptionally large-scale operations during the 18th century. The mines, quarries, mills, and factories of entrepreneurs such as Josse van Robais, the Dutch industrialist brought in by Colbert to produce textiles in Abbeville, only emphasized, by contrast, the primitive conditions of most manufacturing enterprise. Technology relied on limited equipment. Peter the Great saw it at its most impressive when he visited Holland in 1697. In villages along the Zaan River were lumber saws powered by 500 windmills and yards equipped with cranes and stacked with timber cut to set lengths to build *fluitsch-ips* to a standard design.

The typical unit of production, however, was the domestic enterprise, with apprentices and journeymen living with family and servants. The merchant played a vital part in the provision of capital. When metalworkers made knives or needles for a local market, they could remain their own masters. For a larger market, they had to rely on businessmen for fuel, ore, wages, and transport. In textiles the capital and marketing skills of the entrepreneur were essential to cottagers. This putting-out system spread as merchants saw the advantages of evading guild control. When the cotton industry was developed around Rouen and Barcelona, it was organized in the same way as woolen textiles. In the old industrial order, output could be increased only in proportion to the number of workers involved. In England the new order was evolving, and ranks of machines in barrack-like mills were producing for a mass market. The need to produce economically could transform an industry, as in Brabant, where peasants moved into the weaving side of the linen trade and then established bleaching works that ruined traditionally dominant Haarlem. It also altered the social balance, as in electoral Saxony where, between 1550 and 1750, the proportion of peasants who made most of their living by industry rose from 5 to 30 percent of the population. With such change came the dependence on capital and the market that was to make the worker so vulnerable.

Inevitably, the expansion of domestic manufactures brought problems of control, which were eventually resolved by concentration in factories and by technical advances large enough to justify investment in machinery. Starting with the Lombe brothers' silk mills, their exploitation of secrets acquired from Italy (1733), and John Kaye's flying shuttle, British inventions set textile production on a dizzy path of growth. Abraham Darby's process of coke smelting was perhaps the most important single improvement, since it liberated the iron founder from dependence on charcoal. The shortage of timber, a source of anxiety everywhere except in Russia and Scandinavia, proved to be a stimulus to invention and progress. Technical development on the Continent was less remarkable. The nine volumes of the *Theatrum Machinarum* (1724), Jakob Leupold's description of engineering, records steady development reflecting the craftsman's empirical outlook. Improvement could be modest indeed. A miller could grind 37 pounds (17 kg) of flour each day in the 12th century; by 1700 it might have been 55 pounds (25 kg). In some areas there were long intervals between theoretical advances and technological application. Galileo, Evangelista Torricelli, Otto von Guericke, and Blaise Pascal worked on the vacuum in the first half of the 17th century, and Denis Papin later experimented with steam engines; however, it was not until 1711 that Thomas Newcomen produced a model that was of any practical use despite the great need for power. Mining, already well advanced, was held back by difficulties of drainage. In the Rohrerbuhel copper mines in the Tyrol, the Heiliger Geist shaft, at 2,900 feet (886 metres), remained the deepest in the world until 1872; a third of its labour force was employed in draining. Increases in productivity were generally found in those manufacturing activities where, as in the part-time production of linen in Silesia, the skills required were modest and the raw material could be produced locally.

Specialized manufacturing, evolving to meet the rising demand generated by the enrichment of the upper classes, showed significant growth. Wherever technical ingenuity was challenged by the needs of the market, results could be impressive. Printing was of seminal importance, since the advance of knowledge depended

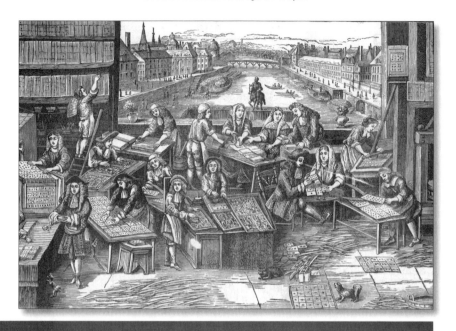

Employees work at a French playing card factory in the 1690s. Hulton
Archive/Getty Images

on it. Improvements in type molds and founding contributed to a threefold increase between 1600 and 1700
in the number of pages printed in a day. The Hollander, a
pulverizing machine (c. 1670), could produce more pulp
for paper than eight stamping mills. The connection
between technical innovation and style is illustrated by
improvements in glassmaking that made possible not
only the casting of large sheets for mirrors but also, by
1700, the larger panes required for the sash windows
that were replacing the leaded panes of casements.
Venice lost its dominant position in the manufacture of
glass as rulers set up works to save expensive imports.
A new product sometimes followed a single discovery,
as when the Saxons Ehrenfried Walter von Tschirnhaus
and Johann Friedrich Böttger successfully imitated
Chinese hard paste and created the porcelain of Meissen.

A way of life could be affected by one invention. The pendulum clock of the Dutch scientist Christiaan Huygens introduced an age of reliable timekeeping. Clocks were produced in great numbers, and Geneva's production of 5,000 timepieces a year was overtaken by 1680 by the clockmakers of both London and Paris. With groups of workers each responsible for a particular task, such as the making of wheels or the decoration of dials, specialization led to enhanced production, and in these elegant products of traditional craftsmanship the division of labour appeared.

CHAPTER 5

THE RISE OF ABSOLUTISM

Among European states of the High Renaissance, the republic of Venice provided the only important exception to princely rule. Following the court of Burgundy, where chivalric ideals vied with the self-indulgence of feast, joust, and hunt, Charles V, Francis I, and Henry VIII acted out the rites of kingship in sumptuous courts. Enormous Poland, particularly during the reign of Sigismund I (1506–48), and the miniature realms of Germany and Italy experienced the same type of regime and subscribed to the same enduring values that were to determine the principles of absolute monarchy. Appeal to God justified the valuable rights that the kings of France and Spain enjoyed over their churches and added sanction to hereditary right and constitutional authority. Henry VIII moved further when he broke with Rome and took to himself complete sovereignty.

Rebellion was always a threat. The skill of Elizabeth I (1558–1603) helped prevent England being torn apart by Roman Catholic and Puritan factions. Philip II (1555–98) failed to repress the continuing rebellion of what became a new state formed out of the northern Burgundian provinces. Neither Charles IX (1560–74) nor Henry III (1574–89) could stop the civil wars in which the Huguenots created an unassailable state within France. The failure of Maximilian I (1493–1519) to implement reforms had left the Holy Roman Empire in poor shape to withstand the religious and political challenges of the Reformation. Such power as Charles V (1519–56) enjoyed in Germany was never enough to do more than contain schism within the bounds confirmed by the Treaty of Augsburg in 1555. Most of Hungary had been lost after the Turkish victory at Mohács in 1526. Imperial authority waned further under Maximilian II (1564–76) and Rudolf II (1576–1612). The terms of Augsburg were flouted as further church lands were secularized and Calvinism gained adherents, some in restless Bohemia. In these ways the stage was set for the subsequent wars and political developments.

With the tendency, characteristic of the Renaissance period, for sovereigns to enlarge their authority and assume new rights in justice and finance, went larger revenues, credit, and patronage. Princes fought with as little regard for economic consequences as their medieval precursors had shown. Ominously, the Italian wars had become part of a larger conflict, centring on the dynastic ambitions of the houses of Habsburg and Valois; similarly, the Reformation led to the formation of alliances whose objectives were not religious. The scale and expertise of diplomacy grew with the pretensions of sovereignty. The professional diplomat and permanent embassy, the regular soldier and standing army, served princes still generally free to act in their traditional spheres. But beyond them, in finance and government, what would be the balance of powers? From the answer to this question will come definition of the absolutism that is commonly seen as characteristic of the age.

The authority of a sovereign was exercised in a society of orders and corporations, each having duties and privileges. St. Paul's image of the Christian body was not difficult for a 17th-century European to understand; the organic society was a commonplace of political debate. The orders, as represented in Estates or diets, were, first, the clergy; second, the nobility (represented with the lords spiritual in the English House of Lords); and, third, commoners. There were variations: upper and lower nobles were sometimes divided; certain towns represented the Third Estate, as in the Castilian Cortes; in Sweden, uniquely, there was an Estate of peasants, whose successful effort to maintain their privilege was one component of Queen Christina's crisis of 1650. When, as in the 16th century, such institutions flourished, Estates were held to represent not the whole population as individuals but the important elements—the "political nation." Even then the nobility tended to dominate. Their claim to represent all who dwelled on their estates was sounder in law and popular understanding than may appear to those accustomed to the idea of individual political rights.

In the empire, the Estates were influential because they controlled the purse. Wherever monarchy was weak in relation to local elites, the diet tended to be used to further their interests. The Cortes of Aragon maintained into the 17th century the virtual immunity from taxation that was a significant factor in Spanish weakness. The strength of the representative institution was proportionate to that of the crown, which depended largely on the conditions of accession. The elective principle might be preserved in form, as in the English coronation service, but generally it had withered as the principle of heredity had been established. Where a succession was disputed, as between branches of the house of Vasa in Sweden after 1595, the need to gain the support of the privileged classes usually led to concessions being made to the body that they controlled. In Poland, where monarchy was elective, the Sejm exercised such power that successive kings, bound by conditions imposed at accession, found it hard to muster forces to defend their frontiers. The constitution remained unshakable even during the reign of John Sobieski (1674–96), hero of the relief of Vienna, who

Soldiers fighting during the Second Siege of Vienna in 1683. Imagno/Hulton Archive/Getty Images

failed to secure the succession of his son. Under the Saxon kings Augustus II (1697–1733) and Augustus III (1734–63), foreign interference led to civil wars, but repeated and factious exercise of the veto rendered abortive all attempts to reform. It required the threat—and in 1772, the reality—of partition to give Stanisław II August Poniatowski (1764–95) sufficient support to effect reforms, but this came too late to save Poland.

At the other extreme were the Russian *zemsky sobor*, which fulfilled a last service to the tsars in expressing the landowners' demand for stricter laws after the disorders of 1648, and the Estates-General of France, where the size of the country meant that rulers preferred to deal with the smaller assemblies of provinces (*pays d'états*) lately incorporated into the realm, such as Languedoc and Brittany. They met regularly and had a permanent staff for raising taxes on property. With respect to the other provinces (*pays d'élection*), the crown had enjoyed the crucial advantage of an annual tax since 1439, when Charles VII successfully asserted the right to levy the personal *taille* without consent. When Cardinal de Richelieu tried to abolish one of the *pays d'état*, the Dauphiné, he met with resistance sufficient to deter him and successive ministers from tampering with this form of fiscal privilege. It survived until the Revolution: to ministers it was a deformity, to critics of the régime it provided at least one guarantee against arbitrary rule. The *zemsky sobor* had always been the creature of the ruler, characteristic of a society that knew nothing of fundamental laws or community rights. When it disappeared, the tsarist government was truly the despotism that the French feared but did not, except in particular cases, experience. When, in 1789, the Estates-General met for the first time since 1614, it abolished the privileged Estates and corporations in the name of the freedom that they had claimed to protect. The age of natural human rights had dawned.

The experience of England, where Parliament played a vital part in the Reformation proceedings of Henry VIII's reign and thus gained in authority, shows that power could be shared between princes and representative bodies. On the Continent it was generally a different story. The Estates-General had been discredited because it had come to be seen as the instrument of faction. Religious differences had stimulated debate about the nature of authority, but extreme interpretations of the right of resistance, such as those that provoked the assassinations of William I the Silent, stadtholder of the Netherlands, in 1584 and Henry III of France in 1589, not only exposed the doctrine of tyrannicide but also pointed to the need for a regime strong enough to impose a religious solution. One such was the Edict of Nantes of 1598, which conceded to the Huguenots not only freedom of worship but also their own schools, law courts, and fortified towns. From the start the Edict constituted a challenge to monarchy and a test of its ability to govern. Richelieu's capture of La Rochelle, the most powerful Huguenot fortress and epicentre of disturbance, after a 14-month siege (1627–28) was therefore a landmark in the making of absolute monarchy, crucial for France and, because of its increasing power, for Europe as a whole.

MAJOR FORMS OF ABSOLUTISM

Absolutism in Europe reached its peak in the 17th and 18th centuries. Possessing complete administrative and military power, an absolute monarch could run his kingdom with individual autonomy or arbitrariness. King Louis XIV of France, the epitome of an absolute monarch, furnished the most familiar assertion of absolutism when he said, "*L'état, c'est moi*" ("I am the state"). In addition to France, the Holy Roman Empire and Prussia were ruled during this period by absolutist sovereigns who exercised virtually unlimited, centralized authority.

In the 18th century the rational ideas of the Enlightenment inspired a version of absolute monarchy called enlightened, or benevolent, despotism. Enlightened despots typically instituted administrative improvements, religious toleration, and economic development, but they did not propose reforms that would undermine their sovereignty or disrupt the social order. Some of the most prominent enlightened despots ruled the Holy Roman Empire and Prussia; among them were the Habsburg monarchs Maria Theresa, Joseph II, and Leopold II, as well as the Prussian king Frederick II.

FRANCE

Certain assumptions influenced the way in which the French state developed. According to the "divine right

Louis XIV

(b. Sept. 5, 1638, Saint-Germain-en-Laye, France—d. Sept. 1, 1715, Versailles)

The king of France from 1643 to 1715, Louis XIV ruled during one of France's most brilliant periods. Known as the Sun King, he remains the preeminent symbol of absolute monarchy. He succeeded his father, Louis XIII, at age four, under the regency of his mother, Anne of Austria. In 1648 the nobles and the Paris Parlement, who hated the prime minister, Cardinal Mazarin, rose against the crown and started the Fronde revolt. In 1653, victorious over the rebels, Mazarin gained absolute power, though the king was of age. In 1660 Louis married Marie-Thérèse of Austria (1638–83), daughter of Philip IV of Spain. When Mazarin died in 1661, Louis astonished his ministers by informing them that he intended to assume responsibility for ruling the kingdom. A believer in dictatorship by divine right, he viewed himself as God's representative on earth. He was assisted by his able ministers, Jean-Baptiste Colbert and the marquis de Louvois. Louis weakened the nobles' power by making them dependent on the crown. A patron of the arts, he protected writers and devoted himself to building splendid palaces, including the extravagant Versailles, where he kept most of the nobility under his watchful eye. In 1667 he invaded the Spanish Netherlands in the War of Devolution (1667–68) and again in 1672 in the Third Dutch War. The Sun King was at his zenith; he had extended France's northern and eastern borders and was adored at his court. In 1680 a scandal involving his mistress, the marchioness de Montespan (1641–1707), made him fearful for his reputation, and he openly renounced pleasure. The queen died in 1683, and he secretly married the pious marchioness de Maintenon. After trying to convert French Protestants by force, he revoked the Edict of Nantes in 1685. Fear of his expansionism led to alliances against France during the War of the Grand Alliance (1688–97) and the War of the Spanish Succession (1701–14). Louis died at age 77 at the end of the longest reign in European history.

Louis XIV of France, "the Sun King." Hulton Archive/Getty Images

of kings" theory, the sovereign held power from God. He ruled in accordance with divine and natural justice and had an obligation to preserve the customary rights and liberties of his subjects. The diversity of laws and taxes meant that royal authority rested on a set of quasi-contractual relationships with the orders and bodies of the realm. Pervading all was a legalistic concern for form, precedence, and the customs that, according to the French jurist Guy Coquille, were the true civil laws. The efforts of successive ministers to create the semblance of a unitary state came less from dogma than from the need to overcome obstacles to government and taxation. Absolutism was never a complete system to match the philosophy and rhetoric that set the king above the law, subject only to God, whom he represented on earth. For 60 years after the Fronde revolt there was no serious challenge to the authority of the crown from either nobles or *parlement*. The idea of divine right, eloquently propounded by Bishop Jacques-Bénigne Bossuet and embodied in the palace and system of Versailles, may have strengthened the political consensus, but it did little to assist royal agents trying to please both Versailles and their own communities. Absolutism on the ground amounted to a series of running battles for political control. In the front line were the *intendants* (administrative officials), first used extensively by Richelieu, then, after their abolition during the Fronde, more systematically and with ever-widening responsibilities, by Louis XIV and his successors until 1789.

Throughout the pre-Revolutionary ancien régime ("old order") the absolutist ideal was flawed, its evolution stunted through persisting contradictions. The fiscal demands of the crown were incompatible with the constant need to stimulate trade and manufacturing enterprise; only a resolute minister operating in peacetime, such as Jean-Baptiste Colbert in the 1660s and Philibert Orry in the

1730s, could hope to achieve significant reforms. There was tension between the Roman Catholic ideal of uniformity and pragmatic views of the state's interest. In 1685 Louis XIV revoked the Edict of Nantes, a harsh if logical resolution of the question. It was what his Catholic subjects expected of him, but it proved damaging to the economy and to France's reputation. A further contradiction lay between measures to overcome the hostility of the nobles to the aggrandizement of the state and the need not to compromise state authority by conceding too much. Richelieu's actions, including the execution of the duc de Montmorency for treason (1632), taught the lesson that no subject was beyond the reach of the law. Louis XIV's brilliant court drew the magnates to Versailles, where social eminence, patronage, and pensions compensated for loss of the power for which they had contended during the Fronde. It merely fortified the regime of privilege that defied fundamental reform to the end. There was another side to the politically advantageous sale of office. Capital was diverted that might better have been employed in business, and there was a vested interest in the status quo. For the mass of the nobility the enlargement of the army, quadrupled in the 17th century, provided an honourable career, but it also encouraged militarism and tempted the king and ministers to neglect the interests of the navy, commerce, and the colonies. When France intervened in the War of the Austrian Succession in 1741, the economic consequences undermined the regime.

The achievements of the Bourbon government, with able ministers working in small, flexible councils, were impressive, even when undermined by weak kings such as Louis XV (1715–74) and Louis XVI (1774–92). In the 18th century, France acquired a fine network of roads, new harbours were built, and trade expanded; a lively culture was promoted by a prosperous bourgeoisie. It may be an irony that the country that nurtured the great thinkers known as the philosophes was the least affected by the reforms they proposed, but it would have been a remarkable king who could have ruled with the courage and wisdom to enable his servants to overcome obstacles to government that were inherent in the system.

THE HOLY ROMAN EMPIRE

The character of Austrian absolutism was derived from a dual situation: with the exception of Maria Theresa, who was debarred by the Salic Law of Succession, the head of the house of Habsburg was also Holy Roman emperor. He directly ruled the family lands, comprising different parts of Austria stretching from Alpine valleys to the Danubian plain, which were mainly Roman Catholic and German; Bohemia, Moravia, and Silesia, which were mainly Slavic in race and language; a fraction of Hungary after the reconquest following the failure of the Turkish Siege of Vienna (1683); and Belgium and Milan (by the Peace of Rastatt in 1714). Each region provided a title and rights pertaining to that state, with an authority limited by the particular rights of its subjects. As an elected emperor, his sovereignty was of a different kind. In effect, the empire was a German confederation, though Bohemia was in and Prussia was outside it; the Mantuan succession affair (1627–31), when the emperor sought to arbitrate, recalls an obsolete Italian dimension. Each German state was self-governing and free to negotiate with foreign powers. Princes, both ecclesiastical and secular, enjoyed the right of representation in the Reichstag (diet). The first of the three *curiae* in the Reichstag was the college of electors, who elected the emperor; the second comprised princes, counts, barons, and the ecclesiastical princes; and the third, the imperial free cities. The 45 dynastic principalities had 80 percent of the land and population; the 60 dynastic counties and lordships comprised only 3 percent. Some of the 60 imperial free cities were but villages. A thousand imperial knights, often landless, each claimed rights of landlordship amounting to sovereignty and owed allegiance only to the emperor in his capacity as president of the Reichstag. Numbers varied through wastage or amalgamation, but they convey the amorphous character of a confederation in which the emperor could only act effectively in concert with the princes, either individually or organized in administrative circles (*Kreis*). Bound by weak ties of allegiance and strong sentiment of nationality, this empire represented the world of medieval universalism with some aspects of the early modern state, without belonging wholly to either. Religious schism had created new frontiers and criteria for policy, such as could justify the elector palatine's decision to accept the crown of Bohemia from the rebels who precipitated the Thirty Years' War. The failure of the emperor Ferdinand II to enlarge his authority or enforce conformity led to the settlements of Westphalia in which his son, Ferdinand III, was forced to concede again the *cuius regio, eius religio* principle. Thereafter he and his successor, Leopold I, devoted their energies to increasing their authority over the family lands. It would be wrong, however, to assume that they, or even the 18th-century emperors, were powerless.

The political climate in which the empire operated was affected by the way universities dominated intellectual life and by trends within universities, in particular the development of doctrines of natural law and cameralism. German rulers respected the universities because the majority of their students became civil servants. With earnest religious spirit went an emphasis on the duty to work and obey. Even in Catholic states the spirit of the Aufklärung (Enlightenment) was pious and practical.

Exponents of natural law, such as the philosopher-scientist
Christian Wolff, advocated religious toleration but saw
no need for constitutional safeguards: the ideal ruler was
absolute. Such commitment to civic virtue explains both
the development of the German state and the survival of
the empire as a working institution. Territorial fragmentation meant a prince's combining his executive role with
that of representative within the Reich (empire): there
could be no stimulus to the development of constitutional
ideas. The German associated political liberty with the
authority of his ruler. He was loyal to his own state, which

Maria Theresa

(b. May 13, 1717, Vienna, Austria—d. Nov. 29, 1780, Vienna)

The wife and empress of the Holy Roman emperor Francis I (reigned
1745–65) and mother of the Holy Roman emperor Joseph II (reigned
1765–90), Maria Theresa was the archduchess of Austria and queen of
Hungary and Bohemia (1740–80) in her own right. She was the eldest
daughter of Emperor Charles VI, who promulgated the Pragmatic
Sanction to allow her to succeed to the Habsburg domains. Opposition
to her succession led in 1740 to the War of the Austrian Succession.
Although the Salic Law of Succession prevented her, as a woman,
from ruling the Holy Roman Empire, after Emperor Charles VII died
(1745), she obtained the imperial crown for her husband, who became
Francis I. She helped initiate financial and educational reforms, promoted commerce and the development of agriculture, and reorganized
the army, all of which strengthened Austria's resources. Continued
conflict with Prussia led to the Seven Years' War and later to the War
of the Bavarian Succession. After her husband's death (1765), her son
became emperor as Joseph II. She criticized many of his actions but
agreed to the partition of Poland (1772). A key figure in the power
politics of 18th-century Europe, Maria Theresa brought unity to the
Habsburg monarchy and was considered one of its most capable rulers. Her 16 children also included Queen Marie-Antoinette of France.

Maria Theresa, Holy Roman empress. Hulton Archive/Getty Images

was the "fatherland"; "abroad" was another state. When judgment was required, the prince would still go to the imperial court, the Reichskammergericht. There were limits to his loyalty. The emperor was expected to lead but could not always do so. So the authorities were ineffective, for example, in the face of Louis XIV's seizure of Strasbourg in 1681. Yet Louis found that German opinion was not to be underestimated; it contributed to his defeat in the War of the Grand Alliance.

Religious animosities persisted into the age of Gottfried Wilhelm Leibniz (1646–1716), but his rational approach and quest for religious unity corresponded to the popular yearning for stability. When interests were so delicately balanced, arbitration was preferable to aggression. The mechanism of the Reichskammergericht saved the counties of Isenburg and Solms from annexation by the ruler of Hesse-Darmstadt. More than a court of law, the Reichskammergericht functioned as a federal executive in matters of police, debts, bankruptcies, and tax claims. Small states such as Mainz could manage their affairs so as to turn enlightened ideas to good use, but was the rulers of the larger states held the keys to Germany's future, and they took note of the emperor; thus his ambivalent position was crucial. Frederick William I of Prussia accepted the ruling of Emperor Charles VI, confirming his right of succession to Berg. In return, the king guaranteed the Pragmatic Sanction, asserting the right of the emperor's daughter to succeed. Charles repudiated Prussia's claim, however, in 1738 when he made a treaty with France. In 1740, when both sovereigns died, Frederick II of Prussia made Austria pay for this slight to his father. The War of the Austrian Succession followed his invasion of Silesia; that valuable Bohemian province remained at the heart of the Austro-Prussian conflict. Its final loss taught Maria Theresa and her advisers, notably Friedrich Haugwitz and

Wenzel von Kaunitz, that they must imitate what they could not defeat. She created, in place of separate Austrian and Bohemian chancelleries, a more effective central administration based on the *Direktorium*, which her son Joseph (coruler from 1765, when he became emperor; sole ruler 1780–90) would develop in ruthless fashion. Maria Theresa respected the Roman Catholic tradition of her house, even while curtailing the powers of the church. Joseph pursued his mother's interests in education and a more productive economy and was concerned with equality of rights and the unity of his domains. Yet he joined in the partition of Poland for the reward of Galicia and showed so little regard for the rules of the empire that he was challenged by Frederick II over the Bavarian succession, which he had sought to manipulate to his advantage. After the ensuing Potato War (1778), the empire's days were numbered, though it required the contemptuous pragmatism of Napoleon to abolish it (1806).

PRUSSIA

King Frederick II of Prussia had inherited a style of absolute government that owed much to the peculiar circumstances of Brandenburg-Prussia as it emerged from the Thirty Years' War. Lacking natural frontiers and war-ravaged when Frederick William inherited the electorate in 1640, Brandenburg had little more than the prestige of the ancient house of Hohenzollern. The diplomacy of Jules Cardinal Mazarin contributed to the acquisition (1648) of East Pomerania, Magdeburg, and Minden, and war between Sweden and Poland brought sovereignty over East Prussia, formerly held as a fief from Poland. A deal with the Junkers at the Recess of 1653, which secured a regular subsidy in return for a guarantee of their social rights, was the foundation of an increasingly absolute rule.

He overcame by force the resistance of the diet of Prussia in 1660: as he became more secure economically, militarily, and bureaucratically, he depended less on his diets. So was established the Prussian model: an aristocracy of service and a bureaucracy harnessed to military needs. Frederick William's son became King Frederick I of Prussia when he pledged support to the emperor's cause (1701). His son, Frederick William I (1713–40), completed the centralization of authority and created an army sustained by careful stewardship of the economy. Personally directing a larger army in wars of aggression and survival, Frederick II the Great (1740–86) came close to ruining his state; its survival

Frederick II

(b. Jan. 24, 1712, Berlin [now in Germany]—d. Aug. 17, 1786, Potsdam, near Berlin)

King Frederick II, known as Frederick the Great, ruled Prussia from 1740 to 1786. The son of Frederick William I, he suffered an unhappy early life, subject to his father's capricious bullying. After trying to escape in 1730, he submitted to his father but continued to pursue intellectual and artistic interests. On his father's death (1740), Frederick became king and asserted his leadership. He seized parts of Silesia during the War of the Austrian Succession, strengthening Prussia considerably. He invaded Saxony in 1756 and marched on into Bohemia. Frederick was almost defeated in the Seven Years' War (1756–63), until his admirer Tsar Peter III signed a Russo-Prussian peace treaty that lasted until 1780. The First Partition of Poland in 1772 led to enormous territorial gains for Prussia. Austro-Prussian rivalry led to the War of the Bavarian Succession (1778–79), a diplomatic victory for Frederick, but continued fear of Habsburg ambitions led him to form a league of German states against Holy Roman emperor Joseph II. Under Frederick's leadership Prussia became one of the great states of Europe, with vastly expanded territories and impressive military strength. In addition to modernizing the army, Frederick also espoused the ideas of enlightened despotism and instituted numerous economic, civil, and social reforms.

King Frederick II of Prussia. Edward Gooch/Hulton Archive/Getty Images

testifies to the success of his father. Of course, Frederick left his own impress on government. He should not be judged by his essays in enlightened philosophy or even by new mechanisms of government, but by the spirit he inspired. He lived out his precept that the sovereign should be the first servant of the state. All was ordered so as to eliminate obstacles to the executive will. Much was achieved: the restoration of Prussia and the establishment of an industrial base, in particular the exploitation of the new Silesian resources. Legal rights and freedom of thought were secure so long as they did not conflict with the interest of the state. A monument to his reign, completed five years after his death in 1786, was the Allgemeine Landrecht, the greatest codification of German law. Perhaps his greatest civil achievement was the stability that made such a striking contrast with the turbulence in Habsburg lands under Joseph II.

VARIATIONS ON THE ABSOLUTIST THEME

The rulers of a variety of other European countries, including Sweden, Denmark, Spain, Portugal, Great Britain, the Netherlands, and Russia, also displayed absolutist characteristics. Some, such as Catherine II of Russia, embraced the theory of enlightened despotism. Yet as the 18th century neared its end, Enlightenment thinking also sparked revolutionary ideas, which ultimately would destroy the foundations of absolute monarchy.

SWEDEN

In Sweden the Konungaförsäkran ("King's Assurance"), which was imposed at the accession of the young Gustav II Adolf in 1611 and which formally made him dependent for all important decisions on the Råd (council) and

Riksdag (diet), was no hindrance to him and his chancellor, Axel Oxenstierna, in executing a bold foreign policy and important domestic reforms. Queen Christina, a minor until 1644, experienced a constitutional crisis (1650) in the aftermath of the Thirty Years' War, from which Sweden had gained German lands, notably West Pomerania and Bremen. She extricated herself with finesse, then abdicated (1654). Charles X sought a military solution to the threat of encirclement by invading Poland and, more successfully, Denmark, but he left the kingdom to his four-year-old son (1660) with problems of political authority unresolved. When he came of age, Charles XI won respect for his courage in war and established an absolutism beyond doubt or precedent by persuading the Riksdag to accept an extreme definition of his powers (1680). Then he carried out the drastic recovery of alienated royal lands. With novel powers went military strength based on a corps of farmer-soldiers from the recovered land. Tempting authority awaited Charles XII (1697–1718), but there was also a menacing coalition. Perhaps decline was inevitable, for Sweden's greatness had been a tour de force, but Charles XII's onslaughts on Poland and Russia risked the state as well as the army which he commanded so brilliantly. Even after the Russian victory at Poltava (1709) and Charles's exile in Turkey, Sweden's resistance testified to the soundness of government. When Charles died fighting in Norway, Sweden had lost its place in Germany and a third of its adult population. An aristocratic reaction led to a period of limited monarchy. Decisions were made by committees of the Riksdag, influenced by party struggle, like that of the Hats and Caps at mid-century. Gustav III carried out a coup in 1774 that restored greater power to the sovereign, but there was no break in two great traditions: conscientious sovereign and responsible nobility.

DENMARK

Denmark also had turned in the absolutist direction. Enforced withdrawal from the Thirty Years' War (in 1629) may not have been a disaster for Denmark, but the loss of the Scanian provinces to Sweden (1658) was—the loss of control of the Sound was a standing temptation to go to war again. Events in Denmark exemplify on a small scale what was happening throughout Europe when princes built from war's wreckage, exploiting the yearning for direction and benefiting from the decay of a society that no longer provided good order. The smaller the country, the stronger the ruler's prospect of asserting his will. As if responding to the English philosopher Thomas Hobbes's formula for absolute monarchy, the Estates declared King Frederick III supreme head on earth, elevated above all human laws (1661). Reforms followed under the statesmen Hannibal Sehested and Peter Schumacker: a new code of law was promulgated; mercantilist measures fostered trade; and Copenhagen flourished. Danes accepted with docility the autocratic rule of the house of Oldenburg, but the peasantry suffered from the spread of a German style of landownership. Frederick IV cared much about their souls, and his son Christian VI provided for their schooling, but a decree of 1733 tied peasants to their estates from the age of 14 to 36. Frederick V was fortunate to have capable ministers, notably Andreas Bernstorff, who was mainly responsible for the acquisition of long-disputed Schleswig and Holstein. His son Christian VII ruled until 1808; yet his reign is best known for his confinement under Johan Struensee and for the latter's liberal reforms. In the two years before his downfall in 1772, more than 1,000 laws were passed, including measures that have left their mark on Danish society to this day. The episode showed the perils as well as benefits of enlightened absolutism when a king or his subject acquired the power to do as he pleased.

SPAIN

The Iberian Peninsula provides further illustration of the absolutist theme. Historians do not agree about the nature or precise extent of Spain's decline, but there is agreement that it did occur and that its causes may be traced not only to the reign of Philip II (1556–98), the overextended champion of Roman Catholic and Spanish hegemony, but also to the social and political structure of the Spanish states of Castile, Aragon, Portugal, Milan, Naples, the Netherlands, and Franche-Comté. The constitutions of these states reflected the personal nature of the original union of crowns (1479) and of subsequent acquisitions. Castile received the largest share of the prosperity that came with silver bullion from the New World but suffered the worst consequences when Mexico and Peru became self-sufficient. Bullion imports fell sharply; trade with the rest of Europe was severely imbalanced; and the weight of taxation fell largely on Castile. The effort of Philip IV's chief minister, the conde de Olivares, to ensure greater equality of contribution through the union of arms was one factor in the revolts of Catalonia and Portugal (1640). In 1659 Spain had to cede Roussillon, Cerdagne, and Artois to France; and in 1667–68 the Flemish forts could put up no fight against the invading French. Despite a partial recovery in the 1680s under the intelligent direction of the duque de Medinaceli and Manuel Oropesa, Spain was the object of humiliating partition treaties. In 1700 Charles II had bequeathed the entire inheritance to Philip of Anjou, Louis XIV's grandson. A foundation for recovery was laid early in the reign of Philip V, when outlying provinces lost their privileges and acquired a tax system based on ability to pay and a French-style *intendente* to enforce it. The pace of reform accelerated with the accession of Charles III in 1759. He was no radical, but he backed ministers who were, such as the conde de Floridablanca and the conde de Campomanes. A national bank, agricultural improvements, and new roads, factories, and hospitals witnessed to the efforts of this benevolent autocrat to overcome the Spanish habit of condemning everything new.

PORTUGAL

Neighbouring Portugal acquired independence in 1668 after revolt and war protracted by the stubborn determination of Philip IV to maintain his patrimony. This small country had suffered since 1580 from its Spanish connection. Resentment at the loss of part of Brazil and most of its Far Eastern colonies had been a major cause of the revolt. The Portuguese did not see their interests as lying with Spain's in partnership with Austria and war against France and Holland. The reorientation of foreign policy and alliance with England by the Methuen Treaty (1703) brought respite rather than restoration. When Sebastien Pombal became the virtual dictator of Portugal as chief minister of Joseph I, he instituted drastic change. If the rebuilding of Lisbon after the great earthquake of 1755 is his memorial, he is also remembered for his assault on the Jesuits; Spain, France, and Austria followed his lead in expelling the powerful religious order, whose grip on education seemed to "enlightened" minds to obstruct progress.

GREAT BRITAIN

The marquês de Pombal was inspired by what he had seen in London, and it was in Great Britain (as it became after the Act of Union between England and Scotland in 1707) that the entrepreneurial spirit was least restricted and most influential in government and society. By the accession of James I in 1603, there had already been a significant divergence from the Continental pattern. The 17th century saw recurring conflict between the crown—more absolute in language than in action—and Parliament. Elected on a narrow, uneven suffrage, it represented privileged interests rather than individuals; it was much concerned with legal precedents and rights. Charles I tried to rule without Parliament from 1629 to 1639, but he alienated powerful interests and, by trying to impose the Anglican prayer book on Scotland, blundered into a civil war that resulted in his overthrow and subsequent execution (1649). Experiments in parliamentary rule culminated in the protectorate of Oliver Cromwell; after his death (1658), Charles II was restored (1660) on financial terms intended to restrict his freedom of maneuver. After a crisis (1678–81) in which the Whigs, led by Lord Shaftesbury, exploited popular prejudice against Roman Catholicism and France to check his absolutist tendency, he recovered the initiative. However, the brief reign of James II (1685–88) justified the fears of those who had sought to exclude him. Policies designed to relieve Roman Catholics antagonized the leaders of the monarchist Anglican church as well as the families who thought that they had the right to manage the state.

The Glorious Revolution brought the Dutch stadtholder to the throne as William III (1689–1702). The intense political struggle left a fund of theory and experience on which 18th-century statesmen could draw. There was, however, no written constitution and only a few statutory limitations. Monarchy retained the power to appoint ministers, make foreign policy, and to manage and direct the army. The Bill of Rights (1689) effectively abolished the suspending and dispensing powers, but William III pursued his European policy with an enlarged army, funded by a new land tax and by loans. Conflict grew between the Whigs and Tories, intensified by the controversy over the War of the Spanish Succession ("Marlborough's war") in the reign of Queen Anne (1702–14). The Triennial Act (1694) ensured elections every three years, and the Act of Settlement (1701) sealed the supremacy of the common law by limiting the king's power to dismiss judges. The accession of George I in 1714 did not lead immediately to stability. The union with Scotland in 1707 had created strains; and Jacobitism remained a threat after the defeat of James Edward Stuart's rising of 1715—until the defeat of his son Charles Edward at Culloden in 1746, it was a focus for the discontented. But investors in government funds had a growing stake in the survival of the dynasty.

When George I gave up attending cabinet meetings, he cleared the way for the Privy Council's displacement by the small cabinet council, and the evolution, in the person of Robert Walpole, first lord of the Treasury from 1721 to 1742, of a "prime minister." Relations between minister and king amounted to a dialogue between the concepts of ministerial responsibility and royal prerogative. Ministers exercised powers legally vested in the monarch; they also were accountable to Parliament. Yet the king could still appoint and dismiss them. Inevitably tensions resulted. The prime minister's right to select fellow ministers did not go unchallenged, but the reluctance of both George I and George II to master the intricacies of patronage, and the skill of Walpole and Newcastle in political management, ensured that the shift in the balance of power in 1688 was irreversible. A centralized legislature coexisted with a decentralized administration. The theme of centre versus provinces, characteristic of other countries, took on a new form as court patronage became the prime element in political management. Most legislation was concerned not with legal or moral principles but with administrative details. Policy tended to emerge from agreement between king and ministers. The royal veto on legislation was never employed after 1708, no government lost a general election, and nearly every Parliament lasted its full term. English philosopher John Locke's dictum that government has no other end but the preservation of property was an apt text for the British political and social system, which was dominated by the church and the aristocracy. Even those 200,000 Englishmen who had the vote could be disfranchised by the common practice of an arranged election. In 1747 only three county and 62 borough elections were contested. The tone was set by the Septennial Act (1716), which doubled the life of Parliaments and the value of patronage.

NETHERLANDS

The English ambassador Sir George Downing in 1664 described the constitution of the United Provinces of the Netherlands, or Dutch Republic, as "such a shattered and divided thing." Louis XIV assumed wrongly, in 1672, that the mercantile republic would prove no match for his armies. Experience had taught the English to respect Dutch naval strength as much as they envied its commercial wealth. Foreign attitudes were ambivalent because this small state was not only the newest but also the richest per capita and quite different from any other. The nation of seamen and merchants was also the nation of painter Rembrandt van Rijn, scientist Christiaan Huygens, and philosopher Benedict de Spinoza; culture and the trading empire were inseparable. After 1572 the Dutch proved that they could hold their own in war. Criticism of the structure of government seems therefore to be wide of the mark. In the development of Amsterdam, private enterprise and civic regulation coexisted in creative harmony; so too the state was effective without impinging on the quality of individual lives. The federal republic, so the

Dutch believed, guarded religion, lands, and liberties. The price was paid by the Spanish southern provinces, which were drained of vitality by emigration to the north, and by the decay of the trade and manufacturing that had given Antwerp a commanding financial position.

The constitution of the United Provinces reflected its Burgundian antecedents in civic pride and its concern for form and precedence. Sovereignty lay with the seven provinces separately; in each the States ruled, and in the States the representatives of the towns were dominant. Since action required a unanimous vote, issues were commonly referred back to town corporations. Only in Friesland did peasants have a voice. The States-General dealt with diplomatic and military measures and with taxes. Its members were ambassadors, closely tied by their instructions. Like contemporary Poles and Germans, the Dutch were separatists at heart, but what was lacking in those countries existed in the United Provinces—one province to lead the rest. Holland assumed, and because of its wealth the rest could not deny, that right. War was again the crucial factor.

One side of the balance was represented by the house of Orange. Maurice of Nassau (1584–1625) and Frederick Henry (1625–47) controlled policy and military campaigns through their virtual monopoly of the office of stadtholder in separate provinces. Monarchs without title, they intermarried with the Protestant dynasties: William III, the grandson of Charles I of England and great-grandson of Henry IV of France, married Mary Stuart and became, with her, joint sovereign of England in 1689. The other side, vigilant for peace, trade, and lower taxes, was represented at its best by Johan de Witt, pensionary of Holland (1653–72). He was murdered during the French invasion of 1672, which brought William III to power. Enlightened oligarchy had little appeal for the poor or tolerance for the Calvinist clergy. Such violence exposed underlying tensions. In 1619 the veteran statesman Johann van Oldenbarneveldt was executed, as much because of the political implications of his liberal stance as for his Arminian views. Holland's open society depended on the commercial values of a magistracy versed in finance and state policy. In 1650 the young stadt-holder William II attempted a coup against Amsterdam, the outcome of which was uncertain. His sudden death settled the issue in favour of a period of rule without stadthold-ers. In 1689 William III's elevation led to consolidation of the republican regime. In 1747, William IV enjoyed popular support for a program of civic reform. As stadtholder of all seven provinces he had concentrated powers, but little was achieved. Not until 1815 was the logical conclusion reached with the establishment of William I as king.

RUSSIA

Successive elective kings of Poland failed to overcome the inherent weaknesses of the state, and the belated reforms of Stanisław II served only to provoke the final dismem-berments of 1793 and 1795. Russia was a prime beneficiary, having long shown that vast size was not incompatible with strong rule. Such an outcome would not have seemed probable in 1648, when revolt in Ukraine led to Russian "protection" and the beginning of that process of expan-sion which was to create an empire. The open character of Russia's boundless lands militated against two processes characteristic of Western society—the growth of cher-ished rights in distinct, rooted communities and that of central authority, adept in the techniques of government. The validity of the state depended on its ability to make the peasant cultivate the soil. If the nobility were to serve the state, they must be served on the land. Serfdom was a logi-cal development in a society that knew nothing of rights. The feudal concept of fealty, the validity of contract, and the idea of liberty as the creation of law were unknown. German immigrants found no provincial Estates, municipal corporations, or craft guilds. Merchants were state functionaries. Absolutism was implicit in the physical conditions and early evolution of Russian society. It could only become a force for building a state comparable to those of the West under a ruler strong enough to challenge traditional ways. This was to be the role of Tsar Alexis I (1645–76) and then, more violently, of Tsar Peter I (1689–1725).

Peter I

(b. June 9, 1672, Moscow, Russia—d. Feb. 8, 1725, St. Petersburg)

Known as Peter the Great, Peter I reigned as tsar of Russia from 1682 to 1725. The son of Tsar Alexis, he reigned jointly with his half brother Ivan V (1682–96) and alone from 1696. Interested in progressive influences from western Europe, he visited several countries there (1697–98). After returning to Russia, he introduced Western technology, modernized the government and military system, and transferred the capital to the new city of St. Petersburg (1703). He further increased the power of the monarchy at the expense of the nobles and the Orthodox church. Some of his reforms were implemented brutally, with considerable loss of life. Suspecting that his son Alexis was conspiring against him, he had Alexis tortured to death in 1718. He pursued foreign policies to give Russia access to the Baltic and Black seas, engaging in war with the Ottoman Empire (1695–96) and with Sweden in the Second Northern War (1700–21). His campaign against Persia (1722–23) secured for Russia the southern and western shores of the Caspian Sea. In 1721 he was proclaimed emperor; his wife succeeded him as the empress Catherine I. For raising Russia to a recognized place among the great European powers, Peter is widely considered one of the outstanding rulers and reformers in Russian history, but he has also been decried by nationalists for discarding much of what was unique in Russian culture, and his legacy has been seen as a model for Joseph Stalin's brutal transformation of Russian life.

Peter I (the Great) of Russia. Rischgitz/Hulton Archive/Getty Images

When the Romanov dynasty emerged in 1613 with
Tsar Michael, the formula for continued power was similar to that of Frederick William, the Great Elector, in
Brandenburg: the common interest of ruler and gentry
enabled Alexis to dispense with the *zemsky sobor*. The great
code of 1649 affirmed the rights of the state over a society that was to be frozen in its existing shape. The tsars
were haunted by the fear that the state would disintegrate.
The acquisition of Ukraine led directly to the revolt of
Stenka Razin (1670), which flared up because of the dis-
content of the serfs. The Russian people had been driven
underground; their passivity could not be assumed. There
was also a threatening religious dimension in the shape
of the Old Believers. Rallying in reaction to the minor
reforms of the patriarch Nikon, they came to express a
general attachment to old Russia. This was as dangerous
to the state when it inspired passive resistance to change
as when it provoked revolt, such as that of the *streltsy*, the
privileged household troops, whom Peter purged in 1698.
Peter's reforms of Russian government must be set against
the military weakness revealed by the Swedish victory at
Narva (1700), the grotesque disorder of government as
exercised by more than 40 councils, the lack of an educated
class of potential bureaucrats, and a primitive economy
untouched by Western technology. His domestic policies
can then be seen as expedients informed by a patchy vision
of Western methods and manners. Catherine II studied
his papers and said, "He did not know what laws were necessary for the state." Yet, without Peter's relentless drive
to create a military power based on compulsory service,
Catherine might have been in no position to carry out any
reforms herself. His Table of Ranks (1722) graded society in
three categories—court, government, and army. The first
eight military grades, all commissioned officers, automati-
cally became gentry. Obligatory service was modified by

later rulers and abolished by Peter III (1762). By then the army had sufficient attraction: the officer caste was secure.

Meanwhile, the bureaucracy exemplified the style of a military police. The uniformed official, rule book in hand, was typical of St. Petersburg government until 1917. Peter's new capital, an outrageous defiance of Muscovite tradition, symbolized the chasm that separated the Westernized elite from the illiterate masses. It housed the senate, set up in 1711, and the nine colleges that replaced the 40 councils. There also was the *oberprokuror*, responsible for the Most Holy Synod, which exercised authority over the church in place of the patriarch. Peter could control the institution; to touch the souls or change the manners of his people was another matter. A Russian was reluctant to lose his beard because God had a beard; a townsman could be executed for leaving his ward; a nobleman could not marry without producing a certificate to show that he could read. With a punitive tax, Peter might persuade Russians to shave and adopt Western breeches and jacket, but he could not trust the free spirit that he admired in England nor expect market, capital, or skills to grow by themselves. So a stream of edicts commanded and explained. State action could be effective—iron foundries, utilizing Russia's greatest natural resource, timber, contributed to the country's favourable trade balance—but nearly all Peter's schools collapsed after his death, and his navy rotted at its moorings.

After Peter there were six rulers in 37 years. Two of the predecessors of Catherine II (1762–95) had been deposed—one of them, her husband Peter III, with her connivance. Along with the instability exemplified by the palace coup of 1741, when the guards regiments brought Elizabeth to the throne, went an aristocratic reaction against centralist government, particularly loathsome as exercised under Anna (1730–40). Elizabeth's tendency to

BEARD CUTTING. A CARICATURE.

This 1705 woodcut was produced by order of Peter the Great to encourage the shaving of beards and to ridicule the Old Believers. The text to the left reads: "Listen, barber, I do not want to be forced to have my beard cut off."
Henry Guttmann/Hulton Archive/Getty Images

delegate power to favoured grandees encouraged aristo-cratic pretension, though it did lead to some enlightened measures.

With the accession of the German-born Catherine, Russians encountered the Enlightenment as a set of ideas and a program of reforms. Since the latter were mostly shelved, questions arise about the sincerity of the royal author of the *Nakaz*, instructions for the members of the Legislative Commission (1767–68). If Catherine still hoped that enlightened reforms, even the abolition of serfdom, were possible after the Commission's muddle, the revolt of Yemelyan Pugachov (1773–75) brought her back to the fundamental questions of security. His challenge to the autocracy was countered by military might, but not before three million peasants had become involved and three thousand officials and gentry had been murdered. The underlying problem remained. The tired soil of old Russia would not long be able to feed the growing population. Trapped between the low yield of agriculture and their ris-ing debts, the gentry wanted to increase dues. The drive for new lands, culminating in the acquisition of the Crimea (1783), increased the difficulties of control. Empirical and authoritarian, Catherine sought to strengthen govern-ment while giving the gentry a share and a voice. The Great Reform of 1775 divided the country into 50 *guberni*. The *dvoriane* were allowed some high posts, by election, on the boards set up to manage local schools and hospitals. They were allowed to meet in assembly. It was more than most French nobles could do: indeed, French demands for assemblies were a prelude to revolution. But as in the case of towns, by the Municipal Reform (1785), she gave only the appearance of self-government. Governors were left with almost unbounded powers. Like Frederick the Great of Prussia, Catherine disappointed the intellectuals, but the development of Russia took place within a framework

Empress Catherine II of Russia, also known as Catherine the Great. Hulton
Archive/Getty Images

of order. European events in the last years of Catherine's life and Russian history, before and since, testify to the magnitude of her achievement.

Absolute monarchy had evolved out of conflicts within and challenges outside the state, notably that of war, whose recurring pressures had a self-reinforcing effect. The absolutist ideal was potent, and the rhetoric voiced genuine feeling. The sovereign who envisaged himself as God's Lieutenant or First Servant of the State was responding to those who had found traditional constitutions wanting and whose Classical education and religious upbringing had schooled them to look for strong rule within a hierarchical system. For more than 150 years, the upper classes of continental Europe were disposed to accept the ethos of absolutism. They would continue to do so only if the tensions within the system could be resolved and if the state were to prove able to accommodate the expectations of the rising bourgeoisie and the potentially unsettling ideas of the Enlightenment.

CHAPTER 6

THE ENLIGHTENMENT

The Enlightenment was both a movement and a state of mind. The term represents a phase in the intellectual history of Europe, but it also serves to define programs of reform in which influential literati, inspired by a common faith in the possibility of a better world, outlined specific targets for criticism and proposals for action. The special significance of the Enlightenment lies in its combination of principle and pragmatism. Consequently, it still engenders controversy about its character and achievements. Two main questions and, relating to each, two schools of thought can be identified. Was the Enlightenment the preserve of an elite, centred on Paris, or a broad current of opinion that the French intellectuals known as the philosophes, to some extent, represented and led? Was it primarily a French movement, having therefore a degree of coherence, or an international phenomenon, having as many facets as there were countries affected? Although most modern interpreters incline to the latter view in both cases, there is still a case for the French emphasis, given the genius of a number of the philosophes and their associates. Unlike other terms applied by historians to describe a phenomenon that they see more clearly than could contemporaries, it was used and cherished by those who believed in the power of mind to liberate and improve. Bernard de Fontenelle, popularizer of the scientific discoveries that contributed to the climate of optimism, wrote in 1702 anticipating "a century which will become more enlightened day by day, so that all previous centuries will be lost in darkness by comparison." Reviewing

the experience in 1784, Immanuel Kant saw an emancipation from superstition and ignorance as having been
the essential characteristic of the Enlightenment.

Before Kant's death, the spirit of the *siècle des
Lumières* ("Age of the Enlightened") had been spurned
by Romantic idealists, its confidence in humans' sense
of what was right and good mocked by revolutionary
terror and dictatorship, and its rationalism decried as
being complacent or downright inhuman. Even its
achievements were critically endangered by the militant
nationalism of the 19th century. Yet much of the tenor of
the Enlightenment did survive in the liberalism, toleration, and respect for law that have persisted in European
society. There was therefore no abrupt end or reversal of
enlightened values.

Nor had there been such a sudden beginning as is
conveyed by the critic Paul Hazard's celebrated apho-
rism: "One moment the French thought like [Bishop
Jacques-Bénigne] Bossuet; the next moment like [the
great Enlightenment writer] Voltaire." The perceptions
and propaganda of the philosophes have led historians
to locate the Age of Reason within the 18th century or,
more comprehensively, between the two revolutions—
England's Glorious Revolution of 1688–89 and the
French Revolution of 1789—but in conception it should
be traced to the humanism of the Renaissance, which
encouraged scholarly interest in Classical texts and values. It was formed by the complementary methods of
the Scientific Revolution, the rational and the empirical. Its adolescence belongs to the two decades before
and after 1700 when writers such as Jonathan Swift were
employing "the artillery of words" to impress the secular intelligentsia created by the growth in affluence,
literacy, and publishing. Ideas and beliefs were tested

wherever reason and research could challenge traditional authority.

SOURCES OF ENLIGHTENMENT THOUGHT

In a cosmopolitan culture, it was the preeminence of
the French language that enabled Frenchmen of the 17th
century to lay the foundations of cultural ascendancy
and encouraged the philosophes to act as the tutors of
18th-century Europe. The notion of a realm of philosophy superior to sectarian or national concerns facilitated
the transmission of ideas. "I flatter myself," wrote Denis
Diderot to the Scottish philosopher David Hume, "that I
am, like you, citizen of the great city of the world." "A philosopher," wrote Edward Gibbon, "may consider Europe as
a great republic, whose various inhabitants have attained
almost the same level of politeness and cultivation." This
magisterial pronouncement by the author of *The Decline
and Fall of the Roman Empire* (1776–88) recalls the common
source: the knowledge of Classical literature.

The scholars of the Enlightenment recognized a joint
inheritance, Christian as well as Classical. In rejecting,
or at least reinterpreting, the one and plundering the
other, they had the confidence of those who believed
they were masters of their destiny. They felt an affinity
with the Classical world and saluted the achievement of
the ancient Greeks, who discovered a regularity in nature
and its governing principle, the reasoning mind, as well as
that of the ancient Romans, who adopted Hellenic culture
while contributing a new order and style: on their law was
founded much of church and civil law. Steeped in the ideas
and language of the classics but unsettled in beliefs, some
Enlightenment thinkers found an alternative to Christian
faith in the form of a neo-paganism. The morality was

based on reason; the literature, art, and architecture were already supplying rules and standards for educated taste.

The first chapter of Voltaire's *Siècle de Louis XIV* specified the "four happy ages": the centuries of Pericles and Plato, of Cicero and Caesar, of the Medicean Renaissance, and, appositely, of Louis XIV. The contrast is with "the ages of belief," which were wretched and backward. Whether denouncing Gothic taste or clerical fanaticism, writers of the Enlightenment constantly resort to images of relapse and revival. Typically, Jean d'Alembert wrote in the *Preliminary Discourse to the Encyclopédie* of a revival of letters, regeneration of ideas, and return to reason and good taste. The philosophes knew enough to be sure that they were entering a new golden age through rediscovery of the old but not enough to have misgivings about a reading of history which, being grounded in a culture that had self-evident value, provided ammunition for the secular crusade.

THE ROLE OF SCIENCE AND MATHEMATICS

"The new philosophy puts all in doubt," wrote the poet John Donne. Early 17th-century poetry and drama abounded in expressions of confusion and dismay about the world, God, and man. The gently questioning essays of the 16th-century French philosopher Michel de Montaigne, musing on human folly and fanaticism, continued to be popular long after his time, for they were no less relevant to the generation that suffered from the Thirty Years' War. Unsettling scientific views were gaining a hold. As the new astronomy of Nicolaus Copernicus and Galileo, with its heliocentric view, was accepted, the firm association between religious beliefs, moral principles, and the traditional scheme of nature was shaken. In this process, mathematics occupied the central position. It was, in the words of René Descartes, "the general science which should explain all that can be known about quantity and measure, considered independently of any application to a particular subject." It enabled its practitioners to bridge gaps between speculation and reasonable certainty: Johannes Kepler thus proceeded from his study of conic sections to the laws of planetary motion. When, however, Fontenelle wrote of Descartes, "Sometimes one man gives the tone to a whole century," it was not merely of his mathematics that he was thinking. It was

René Descartes

(b. March 31, 1596, La Haye, Touraine, France—d. Feb. 11, 1650, Stockholm, Swed.)

The French mathematician, scientist, and philosopher René Descartes is considered the father of modern philosophy. Educated at a Jesuit college, he joined the military in 1618 and traveled widely for the next 10 years. In 1628 he settled in Holland, where he would remain until 1649. Descartes's ambition was to introduce into philosophy the rigour and clarity of mathematics. In his *Meditations on First Philosophy* (1641), he undertook the methodical doubt of all knowledge about which it is possible to be deceived, including knowledge based on authority, the senses, and reason, in order to arrive at something about which he can be absolutely certain; using this point as a foundation, he then sought to construct new and more secure justifications of his belief in the existence and immortality of the soul, the existence of God, and the reality of an external world. This indubitable point is expressed in the dictum *Cogito ergo sum* ("I think, therefore I am"). His metaphysical dualism distinguished radically between mind, the essence of which is thinking, and matter, the essence of which is extension in three dimensions. Though his metaphysics is rationalistic, his physics and physiology are empiricistic and mechanistic. In mathematics, he founded analytic geometry and reformed algebraic notation.

René Descartes, Hulton Archive/Getty Images

the system and philosophy that Descartes derived from the application of mathematical reasoning to the mysteries of the world—all that is meant by Cartesianism—which was so influential. The method expounded in his *Discourse on Method* (1637) was one of doubt: all was uncertain until established by reasoning from self-evident propositions, on principles analogous to those of geometry. It was serviceable in all areas of study. There was a mechanistic model for all living things.

A different track had been pursued by Francis Bacon, the great English lawyer and savant, whose influence eventually proved as great as that of Descartes. He called for a new science, to be based on organized and collaborative experimentation with a systematic recording of results. General laws could be established only when research had produced enough data and then by inductive reasoning, which, as described in his *Novum Organum* (1620), derives from "particulars, rising by a gradual and unbroken ascent, so that it arrives at the most general axioms last of all." These must be tried and proved by further experiments. Bacon's method could lead to the accumulation of knowledge. It also was self-correcting. Indeed, it was in some ways modern in its practical emphasis. Significantly, whereas the devout humanist Thomas More had placed his *Utopia* in a remote setting, Bacon put *New Atlantis* (1627) in the future. "Knowledge is power," he said, perhaps unoriginally but with the conviction that went with a vision of mankind gaining mastery over nature. Thus were established the two poles of scientific endeavour, the rational and the empirical, between which enlightened man was to map the ground for a better world.

Bacon's inductive method is flawed through his insufficient emphasis on hypothesis. Descartes was on strong ground when he maintained that philosophy must proceed from what is definable to what is complex and uncertain.

He wrote in French rather than the customary Latin so as to exploit its value as a vehicle for clear and logical expression and to reach a wider audience. Cartesian rationalism, as applied to theology, for example by Nicholas Malebranche, who set out to refute the pantheism of Benedict de Spinoza, was a powerful solvent of traditional belief: God was made subservient to reason. While Descartes maintained his hold on French opinion, across the English Channel Isaac Newton, a prodigious mathematician and a resourceful and disciplined experimenter, was mounting a crucial challenge. His *Philosophiae Naturalis Principia Mathematica* (1687; *Mathematical Principles of Natural Philosophy*) ranks with the *Discourse on Method* in authority and influence as a peak in the 17th-century quest for truth. Newton did not break completely with Descartes and remained faithful to the latter's fundamental idea of the universe as a machine. But Newton's machine operated according to a series of laws, the essence of which was that the principle of gravitation was everywhere present and efficient. The onus was on the Cartesians to show not only that their mechanics gave a truer explanation but also that their methods were sounder. The Dutch scientist Christiaan Huygens was both a loyal disciple of Descartes and a formidable mathematician and inventor in his own right, who had worked out the first tenable theory of centrifugal force. His dilemma is instructive. He acknowledged that Newton's assumption of forces acting between members of the solar system was justified by the correct conclusions he drew from it, but he would not go on to accept that attraction was affecting every pair of particles, however minute. When Newton identified gravitation as a property inherent in corporeal matter, Huygens thought that absurd and looked for an agent acting constantly according to certain laws. Some believed that Newton was returning to "occult" qualities. Eccentricities apart,

Isaac Newton. Hulton Archive/Getty Images

his views were not easy to grasp; those who actually read the *Principia* found it painfully difficult. Cartesianism was more accessible and appealing.

Gradually, however, Newton's work won understanding. One medium, ironically, was an outstanding textbook of Cartesian physics, Jacques Rohault's *Traité de physique* (1671), with detailed notes setting out Newton's case. In 1732 Pierre-Louis de Mauperthuis put the Cartesians on the defensive by his defense of Newton's right to employ a principle the cause of which was yet unknown. In 1734, in his *Philosophical Letters*, Voltaire introduced Newton as the "destroyer of the system of Descartes." His authority clinched the issue. Newton's physics was justified by its successful application in different fields. The return of Halley's comet was accurately predicted. Charles Coulomb's torsion balance proved that Newton's law of inverse squares was valid for electromagnetic attraction. Cartesianism reduced nature to a set of habits within a world of rules; the new attitude took note of accidents and circumstances. Observation and experiment revealed nature as untidy, unpredictable—a tangle of conflicting forces. In Classical theory, reason was presumed to be common to all human beings and its laws immutable. In Enlightenment Europe, however, there was a growing impatience with systems. The most creative of scientists, such as Robert Boyle, William Harvey, and Antonie van Leeuwenhoek, found sufficient momentum for discovery on science's front line. The controversy was creative because both rational and empirical methods were essential to progress. Like the literary battle between the "ancients" and the "moderns" or the theological battle between Jesuits and Jansenists, the scientific debate was a school of advocacy.

If Newton was supremely important among those who contributed to the climate of the Enlightenment, it is because his new system offered certainties in a world of doubts. The belief spread that Newton had explained forever how the universe worked. This cautious, devout empiricist lent the imprint of genius to the great idea of the Enlightenment: that man, guided by the light of reason, could explain all natural phenomena and could embark on the study of his own place in a world that was no longer mysterious. Yet he might otherwise have been aware more of disintegration than of progress or of theories demolished than of truths established. This was true even within the expanding field of the physical sciences. To gauge the mood of the world of intellect and fashion, of French salons or of such institutions as the Royal Society, it is essential to understand what constituted the crisis in the European mind of the late 17th century.

At the heart of the crisis was the critical examination of Christian faith, its foundations in the Bible, and the authority embodied in the church. In 1647 Pierre Gassendi had revived the atomistic philosophy of Lucretius, as outlined in *On the Nature of Things*. He insisted on the Divine Providence behind Epicurus's atoms and voids. Critical examination could not fail to be unsettling because the Christian view was not confined to questions of personal belief and morals, or even history, but comprehended the entire nature of God's world. The impact of scientific research must be weighed in the wider context of an intellectual revolution. Different kinds of learning were not then as sharply distinguished, because of their appropriate disciplines and terminology, as they are in an age of specialization. At that time philomaths could still be polymaths. Newton's contemporary, Gottfried Wilhelm Leibniz—whose principal contribution to philosophy was that substance exists only in the form of monads, each of which obeys the laws of its own self-determined development while remaining in complete accord with all the rest—influenced his age by concluding that since God contrived the universal harmony this world must be the best of all possible worlds. He also proposed legal reforms, invented a calculating machine, devised a method of the calculus independent of Newton's, improved the drainage of mines, and laboured for the reunification of the Roman Catholic and Lutheran churches.

THE INFLUENCE OF LOCKE

The writing of John Locke, familiar to the French long before the eventual victory of his kind of empiricism, further reveals the range of interests that an educated man might pursue and its value in the outcome: discrimination, shrewdness, and originality. The journal of Locke's travels in France (1675–79) is studded with notes on botany, zoology, medicine, weather, instruments of all kinds, and statistics, especially those concerned with prices and taxes. It is a telling introduction to the world of the Enlightenment, in which the possible was always as important as the ideal and physics could be more important than metaphysics. Locke spent the years from 1683 to 1689 in Holland, in refuge from high royalism. There he associated with other literary exiles, who were united in abhorrence of Louis XIV's religious policies, which culminated in the revocation of the Edict of Nantes (1685) and the flight of more than 200,000 Huguenots. During this time Locke wrote the *Essay on Toleration* (1689). The coincidence of the Huguenot dispersion with the English revolution of 1688–89 meant a cross-fertilizing debate in a society that had lost its bearings. The avant-garde accepted Locke's idea that the people had a sovereign power and that the prince was merely a delegate. His *Second Treatise of Civil Government* (1690) offered a theoretical justification for a contractual view of monarchy on the basis of a revocable agreement between ruler and ruled. It was, however, his writings about education, toleration, and morality that were most influential among the philosophes, for whom his political theories could be only of academic interest. Locke was the first to treat philosophy as purely critical inquiry, having its own problems but essentially similar to other sciences. Voltaire admired what Locke called his "historical plain method" because he had not written "a romance of the soul" but offered "a history of it." The avowed object of his *Essay Concerning Human Understanding* (1690) was "to inquire into the original, certainty, and extent of human knowledge; together with the grounds and degrees of belief, opinion, and assent." For Locke, the mind derives the materials of reason and knowledge from experience. Unlike Descartes's view that man could have innate ideas, in Locke's system knowledge consists of ideas imprinted on the mind through observation of external objects and reflection on the evidence provided by the senses. Moral values, Locke held, are derived from sensations of pleasure or pain, the mind labeling good what experience shows to give pleasure. There are no innate ideas; there is no innate depravity.

Though he suggested that souls were born without the idea of God, Locke did not reject Christianity. Sensationalism, he held, was a God-given principle that if properly followed, would lead to conduct that was ethically sound. He had, however, opened a way to disciples who proceeded to conclusions that might have been far from the master's mind. One such was the Irish bishop George Berkeley who affirmed, in his *Treatise on the Principles of Human Knowledge* (1710), that there was no proof that matter existed beyond the idea of it in the mind. Most philosophers after Descartes decided the question of the dualism of mind and matter by adopting a materialist position; whereas they eliminated mind, Berkeley eliminated matter—and he was therefore neglected. Locke was perhaps more scientific and certainly more in tune with the intellectual and practical concerns of the age. Voltaire presented Locke as the advocate of rational faith and of sensationalist psychology; Locke's posthumous success was assured. In the debate over moral values, Locke provided a new argument for toleration. Beliefs, like other human differences, were largely the product of environment. Did it not therefore follow that moral improvement should be the responsibility of society? Finally, since human irrationality was the consequence of false ideas, instilled by faulty schooling, should not education be a prime concern of rulers? To pose those questions is to anticipate the agenda of the Enlightenment.

THE PROTO-ENLIGHTENMENT

If Locke was the most influential philosopher in the swirling debates of late-17th-century Holland, the most prolific writer and educator was Pierre Bayle, whom Voltaire called "the first of the skeptical philosophers." He might also be called the first of the encyclopaedists, for he was more publicist than philosopher, eclectic in his interests, information, and ideas. The title *Nouvelles de la république des lettres* (1684–87) conveys the method and ideal of this superior form of journalism. Bayle's *Historical Dictionary* (1697) exposed the fallacies and deceits of the past by the plausible method of biographical articles. "The grounds of doubting are themselves doubtful; we must therefore doubt whether we ought to doubt." Lacking a sound criterion of truth or a system by which evidence could be tested but hating dogma and mistrusting authority, Bayle was concerned with the present state of knowledge. He may have been as much concerned with exposing the limitations of human reason as with attacking superstition.

Translated and abridged, as, for example, by order of Frederick II of Prussia, the *Dictionary* became the skeptic's bible. The effect of Bayle's work and that of others less scrupulous, pouring from the presses of the Netherlands and Rhineland and easily penetrating French censorship, could not fail to be broadly subversive.

Bayle's seminal role in the cultural exchange of his time points to the importance of the Dutch Republic in the 17th century. Because Holland contributed little to science, philosophy, or even art at the time of the philosophes, though enviable enough in the tranquil lives of many of its citizens, its golden 17th century tends to be overlooked in traditional accounts of the Enlightenment. Wealth derived from trade, shipping, and finance and the toleration that attracted Sephardic Jews, Protestants from Flanders and France, and other refugees or simply those who sought a relatively open society combined to create a climate singularly favourable to enterprise and creativity. It was urban, centring on Amsterdam, and it was characterized by a rich artistic life created by painters who worked to please patrons who shared their values. It was pervaded by a scientific spirit. Pieter de Hooch's search for new ways of portraying light, Spinoza's pursuit of a rational system that would comprehend all spiritual truth. Leeuwenhoek's use of the microscope to reveal the hidden and minute, Hermann Boerhaave's dissection of the human corpse, Jan Blaeuw's accuracy in the making of maps, and Huygens's precise measurement of time in the new pendulum clock—each represents that passion for discovery that put 17th-century Holland in a central position between the Renaissance and the Enlightenment, with some of the creative traits of both periods. Its spirit is epitomized in the State University of Leiden, which attracted students from throughout Europe by its excellence in medicine and law and its relative freedom from ecclesiastical authority.

It was fitting, therefore, that much of the writing that helped form the Enlightenment emanated from the printing presses of the Huguenot emigré Louis Elsevier at Amsterdam and Leiden. Bayle's skepticism belongs to the time when dust was still rising from the collapsing structures of the past, obscuring such patterns of thought as would eventually emerge. There was no lack of material for them. Not only did learning flourish in the cultural common market that served the needs of those who led or followed intellectual fashions; also important, though harder to measure, was the influence of the new relativism, grounded in observable facts about an ever-widening world. It was corrosive alike of Cartesian method, Classical regulation, and traditional theology. Of Descartes, Huygens had written that he had substituted for old ideas "causes for which one can comprehend all that there is in nature."

Allied to that confidence in the power of reason was a prejudice against knowledge that might distort argument. Blaise Pascal had perfectly exemplified that rationalist frame of mind prone to introspection, which in his case— that of mathematical genius and literary sensibility in rare combination—produced some of the finest writing of his day. But the author of the *Pensées* (1669) was reluctant to travel: "All the ills that affect a man proceed from one cause, namely that he has not learned to sit quietly and contentedly in one room." Again, the object of the protagonists of the prevailing classicism had been to establish rules: for language (the main role of the French Academy), for painting (as in the work of Nicolas Poussin), even for the theatre, where Jean Racine's plays of heightened feeling and pure conflict of ideal or personality gain effect by being constrained within the framework of their Greek archetypes.

HISTORY AND SOCIAL THOUGHT

Order, purity, clarity: such were the Classical ideals. They had dominated traditional theology as represented by its last great master, Jacques-Bénigne Bossuet. His *Politique tirée des propres paroles de l'Écriture sainte* ("Statecraft Drawn from the Very Words of the Holy Scriptures") and *Discours sur l'histoire universelle* offered a worldview and a history based on the Old Testament. Bossuet believed in the unity of knowledge as so many branches of Christian truth. His compelling logic and magisterial writing had a strong influence. When, however, the hypotheses were tested and found wanting, the very comprehensiveness of the system ensured that its collapse was complete. Bossuet had encouraged Richard Simon when he set out to refute Protestantism through historical study of the Bible but was shocked when he saw where it led. Inevitably, scholarship revealed inconsistencies and raised questions about the way that the Bible should be treated: if unreliable as history, then how sound was the basis for theology? Simon's works were banned in 1678, but Dutch printers ensured their circulation. No censorship could prevent the development of historical method, which was making a place for itself in the comprehensive search for truth. With Edward Gibbon (himself following the example of the 17th-century giants of church history), Jean Mabillon, and Louis Tillemont, historians were to become more skilled and scrupulous in the use of evidence. The philosophes characteristically believed that history was becoming a science because it was subject to philosophical method. It also was subject to the prevailing materialist bias, which is why, scholarly though individual writers like David Hume might be, the Enlightenment was in some respects vulnerable to fresh insights about man—such as those of Étienne Bonnot de Condillac, who believed that human beings could be molded for their own good—and further research into the past—which, for Claude-Adrien Helvétius, was simply the worthless veneration of ancient laws and customs.

In 1703 the baron de Lahontan introduced the idea of the "noble savage," who led a moral life in the light of natural religion. In relative terms, the uniquely God-given character of European values was questioned; Louis XIV's persecution of the Huguenots and Jansenists offered an unappealing example. Philosophers were provided, through the device of *voyages imaginaires*, with new insights and standards of reference. As Archbishop Fénelon was to show in *Télémaque* (1699)—where the population of his imaginary republic of Salente was engaged in farming and the ruler, renouncing war, sought to increase the wealth of the kingdom—a utopian idyll could be a vehicle for criticism of contemporary institutions. A bishop and sentimental aristocrat, heir to the tradition of Christian agrarianism, might seem an unlikely figure to appear in the pantheon of the Enlightenment. But his readers encountered views about the obligations as well as rights of subjects that plainly anticipate its universalism, as in the *Dialogue des morts*: "Each individual owes incomparably more to the human race, the great fatherland, than to the country in which he is born."

THE LANGUAGE OF THE ENLIGHTENMENT

It is easier to identify intellectual trends than to define enlightened views, even where, as in France, there was a distinct and self-conscious movement, which had by mid-century the characteristics of a party. Clues can be found in the use commonly made of certain closely related cult words such as Reason, Nature, and Providence. From

having a sharp, almost technical sense in the work of
Descartes, Pascal, and Spinoza, reason came to mean
something like common sense, along with strongly pejo-
rative assumptions about things not reasonable. For
Voltaire, the reasonable were those who believed in
progress: he lived "in curious times and amid astonish-
ing contrasts: reason on the one hand, the most absurd
fanaticism on the other." Nature in the post-Newtonian
world became a system of intelligible forces that grew as
the complexity of matter was explored and the diversity
of particular species discovered. It led to the pantheism
of the Irish writer John Toland, for whom nature replaced
God, and to the absolute doubt of Julien La Mettrie, who
in *L'Homme machine* (1747) took the position that nothing
about nature or its causes was known. In England, in the
writing of Lord Shaftesbury and David Hartley, nature
served the cause of sound morals and rational faith. One
of the foremost theologians, Joseph Butler, author of
the *Analogy of Religion* (1736), tested revelation against
nature and in so doing erased the troublesome distinction in a manner wholly satisfying to those who looked
for assurance that God could be active in the world without breaking the laws of its being. Finally, to Jean-Jacques
Rousseau, nature—the word that had proved so useful to
advocates of an undogmatic faith, of universal principles
of law or even, in the hands of the physiocrats, the "natural," or market, economy—acquired a new resonance. In
his *Discourse on the Origin of Inequality* (1755), he wrote:
"We cannot desire or fear anything, except from the idea
of it, or from the simple impulse of nature." Nature had
become the primal condition of innocence in which man
was whole—not perfect, but imbued with virtues that
reflected the absence of restraints.

Along with the new view of the universe grew belief in
the idea of a benign Providence, which could be trusted

because it was visibly active in the world. Writers sought to express their sense of God's benevolent intention as manifest in creation. To the French clergyman known as the abbé Pluche, domestic animals were not merely docile but naturally loved humanity. Voltaire, equally implausibly, observed of mountain ranges that they were "a chain of high and continuous aqueducts which, by their apertures allow the rivers and arms of the sea the space which they need to irrigate the land." The idea of Providence could degenerate into the fatuous complacency that Voltaire himself was to deride and against which—in particular, the idea that the universe was just a vast theatre for the divine message—Samuel Taylor Coleridge was memorably to rebel. Faith, wrote the English poet, "could not be intellectually more evident without being morally less effective; without counteracting its own end by sacrificing the life of faith to the cold mechanism of a worthless because compulsory assent." So the Enlightenment can be seen to be carrying the seeds of its own disintegration. The providential idea was based on unscientific assumptions in an age in which scientists, favoured by a truce with men of religion, were free to pursue researches that revealed an untidier, therefore less comforting, world. Newton had argued, from such problems as irregularities in the orbit of planets, that divine intervention was necessary to keep the solar system operating regularly. D'Alembert found, however, that such problems were self-correcting. From being the divine mechanic had God now become the divine spectator?

No less unsettling were the findings of geologists. Jean-Étienne Guettard concluded that the evidence of fossils found in the volcanic hills of the Puy de Dôme in south-central France conflicted with the time scheme of the Old Testament. Whether, like the French naturalist Georges-Louis Leclerc, comte de Buffon, they attributed

Scottish Enlightenment

The conjunction of minds, ideas, and publications in Scotland during the whole of the second half of the 18th century and extending over several decades on either side of that period is known as the Scottish Enlightenment. Contemporaries referred to Edinburgh as a "hotbed of genius." Voltaire in 1762 wrote in characteristically provocative

David Hume, oil painting by Allan Ramsay, 1766; in the Scottish National Portrait Gallery, Edinburgh. Courtesy of the Scottish National Portrait Gallery

fashion that "today it is from Scotland that we get rules of taste in all the arts, from epic poetry to gardening," and Benjamin Franklin caught the mood of the place in his *Autobiography* (1794): "Persons of good Sense ... seldom fall into [disputation], except Lawyers, University Men, and Men of all Sorts that have been bred at Edinburgh."

France and England supplied the sources of some of the ideas that were absorbed by Edinburgh, but the pot in which they were cooked had a distinctive quality and history. The Enlightenment in Scotland did not draw upon aristocratic patronage as did its counterpart in France. The driving forces were, on the one hand, a remarkably well-educated population (a legacy of the Reformation in Scotland) and, on the other, the absence of what gave form and direction to English society—a long-developed history of authority being derived from a common-law system based upon tradition and precedent. There was no such history in Scotland.

The personalities were fundamental to the Scottish Enlightenment: most prominent in retrospect are the philosophers David Hume and Adam Smith. However, the Scottish Enlightenment was neither

Scientist Joseph Black visiting inventor James Watt in his University of Glasgow workshop. © Photos.com/Jupiterimages

a single school of philosophical thought nor a single intellectual movement. It was a movement of taste in architecture, in literature and belles lettres, and in the arts, especially in portraiture. Equally central were those who made lasting and formative impacts on the development of the sciences of mathematics, medicine, chemistry, engineering, and geology.

to matter a form of life, speculated about life as a constant, shapeless flux, or postulated a history of the world that had evolved over an immensely long time, scientists were dispensing with God as a necessary factor in their calculations. Some theologians sought compromise, while others retreated, looking to a separate world of intuitive understanding for the justification of faith. Joseph Butler pointed to conscience, the voice of God speaking to the human soul. He deplored the enthusiasm that characterized the tireless preaching of John Wesley and his message of the love of God manifested in Christ. "A true and living faith in God," Butler declared, "is inseparable from a sense of pardon from all past and freedom from all present sins." It was not the freedom understood by the philosophes, but it touched hearts and altered lives. Meanwhile the path of reason was open for the avowed atheism of Baron d'Holbach, who declared in his *Système de la nature* (1770; "The System of Nature") that there was no divine purpose: "The whole cannot have an object for outside itself there is nothing towards which it can tend." Another approach was taken by David Hume, author of *Treatise on Human Nature* (1739) and the *Dialogues Concerning Natural Religion* (1779). The notion of miracles was repugnant to reason, but he was content to leave religion as a mystery, to be a skeptic about skepticism, and to deny that man could reach objective knowledge of any kind.

These may appear to have been intellectual games for the few. It could only be a privileged, relatively leisured minority, even among the educated, who actively participated in debate or could even follow the reasoning. The impact was delayed; it was also uneven. In Samuel Johnson's England the independence bestowed by the Anglican clergyman's freehold and the willingness of the established church to countenance rational theology created a shock absorber in the form of the Broad Church. In Protestant countries criticism tended to be directed toward amending existing structures: there was a pious as well as an impious Enlightenment. Among Roman Catholic countries France's situation was in some ways unique. Even there orthodox doctrines remained entrenched in such institutions as the Sorbonne; some bishops might be worldly but others were conscientious; monasteries decayed but parish life was vital and curés (parish priests) well trained. Nor was theology neglected: in 1770, French publishers brought out 70 books in defense of the faith. Of course the philosophes, endowed with the talents and the means to mount sustained campaigns, ensured that the question of religion remained high on the agenda. There was also a ready sale for writers who sought to apply the rational and experimental methods to what Hume was to call the science of man.

THE INDIVIDUAL AND SOCIETY

Chief among the writers who examined the individual's relationship to society was Charles de Secondat de Montesquieu. His presidency in the *parlement* of Bordeaux supported the career of a litterateur, scholarly but shrewd in judgment of men and issues. In the *Persian Letters* (1721), he had used the supposed correspondence of a Persian visitor to Paris to satirize both the church (under

that "magician" the pope) and the society upon which it
appeared to impose so fraudulently. His masterpiece, *The
Spirit of Laws*, appeared in 22 editions within 18 months
of publication in 1748. For this historically minded lawyer, laws were not abstract rules but were necessary
relationships derived from nature. Accepting completely
Locke's sensationalist psychology, he pursued the line
of the Sicilian Giambattista Vico, the innovative author
of *The New Science* (1725), toward the idea that human
values are the evolving product of society itself. Among
social factors, he listed climate, religion, laws, the principles of government, the example of the past, and social
practices and manners and concluded that from these
a general spirit is formed. Montesquieu's concern with
knowledge as a factor in shaping society is characteristic
of the Enlightenment. Nor was he alone in his Anglophile
tendency, though it did not prevent him from misinter-
preting the English constitution as being based on the
separation of powers. The idea that moral freedom could
be realized only in a regime whose laws were enacted by
an elected legislature, administered by a separate executive, and enforced by an independent judiciary was to be
more influential in the New World than in the Old. His
theories reflected a Newtonian view of the static equilib-
rium of forces and were influenced by his perception of
the French government as increasingly arbitrary and centralist; they were conceived as much as a safeguard against
despotism as an instrument of progress.

Montesquieu's political conservatism belonged to a
world different from that of the younger generation of
philosophes, for whom the main obstacle to progress was
privilege; they put their trust in "the enlightened autocrat"
and in his mandate for social engineering. They might fear,
like Claude Helvétius, that his theories would please the aristocracy. Helvétius—a financier, amateur philosopher, and

author of the influential *De l'esprit* (1759; "On the Mind") —
advocated enlightened self-interest in a way that found an
echo in physiocratic economic theory and argued that each
individual, in seeking his own good, contributed to the general good. Laws, being man-made, should be changed so as
to be more useful. The spirit of the Enlightenment is well
conveyed by his suggestion that experimental ethics should
be constructed in the same way as experimental physics.
By contrast, Montesquieu, whose special concern was the
sanctity of human law, saw the problem of right conduct
as one of adapting to circumstances. The function of reason was to bring about accord between human and natural
law. While the objective nature of his inquiry encouraged
those who trusted in the power of reason to solve human
problems, it was left to those who saw the Enlightenment
in more positive terms to work for change.

François-Marie Arouet, whose nom de plume of Voltaire
was to become almost synonymous with the Enlightenment,
was a pupil of the Jesuits at their celebrated college of
Louis-le-Grand; his political education included 11 months
in the Bastille prison. The contrast between the arbitrary
injustice epitomized by the lettre de cachet (a letter signed
by the king that authorized imprisonment) that brought
about his imprisonment, without trial, for insulting a
nobleman and the free society he subsequently enjoyed in
England was to inspire a life's commitment to the principles
of reason, liberty, justice, and toleration. Voltaire at times
played the role of adviser to princes (notably Frederick II
of Prussia) but learned that it was easier to criticize than to
change institutions and laws. Like other philosophes living
under a regime that denied political opportunity, he was no
politician. Nor was he truly a philosopher in the way that
Locke, Hume, or even Montesquieu can be so described.
His importance was primarily as an advocate at the bar of
public opinion. The case for the reform of archaic laws and

the war against superstition was presented with passion and authority, as notably in his *Philosophical Dictionary*. *Candide* (1759) shows his elegant command of language, whose potential for satire and argument had been demonstrated by Pascal's *Provincial Letters* of a century before. With astute judgment, he worked on the reader's sensibilities. "The most useful books," he wrote, "are those to which the readers themselves contribute half; they develop the idea of which the author has presented the seed." He could lift an episode—the execution of Admiral Byng (1757) for failing to win a battle; of Jean Calas, seemingly, for being a Huguenot (1762); or of the Chevalier de la Barre, after torture, for alleged blasphemy (1766)—to the level at which it exemplified the injustices committed when man would not listen to the voice of reason or could not do so because of archaic laws. In *Candide*, he presented the debate between the optimistic Dr. Pangloss and Martin, who believes in the reality of evil, in a way that highlights the issues and is as significant now as then.

Voltaire mounted his campaigns from a comfortable base, his large estate at Ferney. He was vain enough to relish his status as a literary lion and freedom's champion. He could be vindictive and was often impatient with differing views. In his reluctance to follow ideas through or consider their practical implications and in his patrician disregard for the material concerns of ordinary people, he epitomized faults with which the philosophes can be charged, the more so because they were so censorious of others. He was generous chiefly in imaginative energy, in the indignation expressed in the celebrated war cry "*Écrasez l'infâme*" (literally "crush infamy," signifying for Voltaire the intolerance of the church), and in the time he devoted to the causes of wronged individuals with whose plight he could identify. He had little to put in place of the religion he abused and offered no alternative vision. He did succeed notably in making people think about important questions — indeed, his questions were usually clearer than his answers.

THE *ENCYCLOPÉDIE*

The marquis de Condorcet, a mathematician and one of the more radical of his group, described his fellow philosophes as "a class of men less concerned with discovering truth than with propagating it." That was the spirit which animated the great *Encyclopédie*, the most ambitious publishing enterprise of the century. It appeared in 17 volumes between 1751 and 1765, after checks and delays that would have disheartened anyone less committed than its publisher, André-François le Breton, or its chief editor and presiding genius, Denis Diderot. Its publishing history is rich in incident and in what it reveals of the ambience of the Enlightenment. The critical point was reached in 1759, when French defeats made the authorities sensitive to anything that implied criticism of the regime. The publication of Helvétius's *De l'esprit*, together with doubts about the orthodoxy of another contributor, the abbé de Prades, and concern about the growth of Freemasonry, convinced government ministers that they faced a plot to subvert authority. If they had been as united as the officials of the church, the *Encyclopédie* would have been throttled. It was placed on the Index of Forbidden Books, and a ban of excommunication was pronounced on any who should read it; but even Rome was equivocal. The knowledge that Pope Benedict XIV was privately sympathetic lessened the impact of the ban; Chrétien Guillaume de Lamoignon de Malesherbes, from 1750 to 1763 *directeur de la librairie* (director of the press), whose sanction was required for publication, eased the passage of volumes he was supposed to censor. Production continued, but without Rousseau, an early contributor, who became increasingly hostile to the encyclopaedists and their utilitarian philosophy.

Diderot's coeditor, the mathematician Jean le Rond d'Alembert, had, in his preface, presented history as the record of progress through learning. The title page proclaimed the authors' intention to outline the present state of knowledge about the sciences, arts, and crafts. Among its contributors were craftsmen who provided the details for the technical articles. Pervading all was Diderot's moral theme: through knowledge "our children, better instructed than we, may at the same time become more virtuous and happy." Such utilitarianism, closely related to Locke's environmentalism, was one aspect of what d'Alembert called "the philosophic spirit." If it had been only that, it would have been as useful as Ephraim Chambers's *Cyclopaedia* (1727), which it set out to emulate. Instead, it became the textbook for the thoughtful—predominantly office-holders, professionals, the bourgeoisie, and particularly the young, who might appreciate Diderot's idea of the *Encyclopédie* as the means by which to change the common way of thinking. In the cause, Diderot sustained imprisonment in the jail at Vincennes (1749) and had to endure the condemnation and burning of one of his books, *Philosophic Thoughts* (1746). There was nothing narrow about his secular mission. *Pensées sur l'interprétation de la nature* (1753) advanced the idea of nature as a creative process of which man was an integral part. But his greatest achievement was the *Encyclopédie*, Most of the important thinkers of the time contributed to it. Differences were to be expected, but there was enough unanimity in principles to endow the new gospel of scientific empiricism with the authority that Scripture was losing. It was also to provide a unique source for reformers. Catherine II of Russia wrote to the German critic Friedrich Melchior Grimm for suggestions as to a system of education for young people. Meanwhile, she said she would "flip through the *Encyclopédie*; I shall certainly find in it everything I should and should not do."

ROUSSEAU AND HIS FOLLOWERS

Diderot prefigured the unconventional style that found its archetype in Jean-Jacques Rousseau. In his novel of the 1760s, *Rameau's Nephew*, Diderot's eccentric hero persuades his bourgeois uncle, who professes virtue, to confess to actions so cynical as to be a complete reversal of accepted values. Rousseau was close to this stance when he ridiculed those who derived right action from right thinking. He understood the interests of the people, which the philosophes tended to neglect and which Thomas Paine considered in the *Rights of Man* (1791). If virtue were dependent on culture and culture the prerogative of a privileged minority, what was the prospect for the rest: "We have physicians, geometricians, chemists, astronomers, poets, musicians and painters in plenty; but no longer a citizen among us." Rousseau is thus of the Enlightenment yet against it, at least as represented by the mechanistic determinism of Condillac or the elitism of Diderot, who boasted that he wrote only for those to whom he could talk—i.e., for philosophers. Rousseau challenged the privileged republic of letters, its premises, and its principles. His *Confessions* depicted a well-intentioned man forced to become a rogue and outcast by the artificiality of society. His first essay, *Discourse on the Arts and Sciences* (1750), suggested the contradiction between the exterior world of appearances and the inner world of feeling. With his view of culture now went emphasis on the value of emotions. Seminal use of concepts—such as "citizen" to indicate the rights proper to a member of a free society—strengthened signals that could otherwise confuse as much as inspire.

Dealing with the basic relations of life, Rousseau introduced the prophetic note that was to sound through

Jean-Jacques Rousseau. Hulton Archive/Getty Images

democratic rhetoric. The state of nature was a hypothesis rather than an ideal: man must seek to recover wholeness at a higher level of existence. For this to be possible he must have a new kind of education and humanity a new political constitution. *Émile* (1762) proposed an education to foster natural growth. His *Social Contract* (1762) was banned, and this lent glamour to proposals for a constitution to enable the individual to develop without offending against the principle of social equality. The crucial question concerned legitimate authority. Rousseau rejected both natural law and force as its basis. He sought a form of association that would allow both security and the natural freedom in which "each man, giving himself to all, gives himself to nobody." It is realized in the form of the general will, expressed in laws to which all submit. More than the sum of individual wills, it is general in that it represents the public spirit seeking the common good, which Rousseau defined as liberty and equality, the latter because liberty cannot subsist without it. He advocated the total sovereignty of the state, a political formula which depended on the assumption that the state would be guided by the general will. Rousseau's good society was a democratic and egalitarian republic. Geneva, his birthplace, was to prove boundless in inspiration. Rousseau's influence may have been slight in his lifetime, though some were proud to be numbered among admirers. His eloquence touched men of sensibility on both sides of the Atlantic.

The French writer Morelly in the *Code de la nature* (1755), attacked property as the parent of crime and proposed that every man should contribute according to ability and receive according to need. Two decades later, another radical clergyman, Gabriel de Mably, started with equality as the law of nature and argued that the introduction of property had destroyed the golden age of man. In England, William Godwin, following Holbach in obeisance to reason, condemned not only property but even the state of marriage: according to Godwin, man freed from the ties of custom and authority could devote himself to the pursuit of universal benevolence. To the young poets William Wordsworth and Percy Bysshe Shelley it was a beguiling vision; those less radical might fear for social consequences, such as the French draftsmen of the Declaration of the Rights of Man and of the Citizen of 1789, who were careful to proclaim the sacred right of property. Thomas Jefferson made the rights of man the foundation of his political philosophy as well as of the U.S. Constitution, but he remained a slave owner. The idea of "de-natured" man was as potent for the unsettling of the ancien régime as loss of the sense of God had been for the generation of Martin Luther and Ignatius Loyola. It struck home to the educated young who might identify with Rousseau's self-estrangement and read into the image of "man everywhere in chains" their own perception of the privilege that thwarted talent. Such were Maximilien Robespierre, the young lawyer of Arras; Aleksandr Radischev, who advocated the emancipation of Russian serfs, or the Germans who felt restricted in regimented, often minuscule states. Both the severe rationalism of Kant and the idealism of Sturm und Drang (German: "Storm and Stress"; a literary movement of the late 18th century that exalted nature, feeling, and human individualism) found inspiration in Rousseau. Yet Kant's *Critique of Pure Reason* (1781) and the sentimental hero portrayed by Johann Wolfgang von Goethe in his *Sorrows of Young Werther* (1774) mark the end of the Enlightenment. "It came upon us so gray, so cimmerian, so corpse-like that we could hardly endure its ghost," wrote Goethe, speaking for the Romantic generation and pronouncing valediction.

In France, the Enlightenment touched government circles only through individuals, such as Anne-Robert Turgot, a physiocrat, finance minister (1774–76), and frustrated reformer. The physiocrats, taking their cue from such writers as François Quesnay, author of *Tableau économique* (1758), advocated the removal of artificial obstacles to the growth of the natural economic order of a free market for the produce of the land. Even Adam Smith, who wrote the *Wealth of Nations* (1776) with a capitalist economy in mind, could see his avowed disciple William Pitt move only cautiously in the direction of free trade. Though the visionary William Blake could be adduced to show that there was powerful resistance to the new industrial society, the physician and scientist Erasmus Darwin was—with his fellow luminaries of the Lunar Society, Josiah Wedgwood and Matthew Boulton—at the heart of the entrepreneurial culture: there was no deep divide separating the English philosophes, with their sanctification of private property and individual interests, from the values and programs of government. In *dirigiste* France, where there was no internal common market and much to inhibit private investment, physiocratic ideas were politically naive: the gap between theory and implementation only illustrates the way in which the Enlightenment undermined confidence in the regime. Operating in a political vacuum, the philosophes could only hope that they would, like Diderot with Catherine the Great, exercise such influence abroad as might fulfill their sense of mission. In both Germany and Italy, however, circumstances favoured emphasis on the practical reforms that appealed as much to the rulers as to their advisers.

THE ENLIGHTENMENT IN GERMANY

In Germany the Enlightenment, known there as the Aufklärung, found its highest expression in a science of government. One explanation lies in the importance of universities. There were nearly 50 by 1800 (24 founded since 1600); they were usually the product of a prince's need to have trained civil servants rather than of a patron's zeal for higher learning. Not all were as vigorous as Halle (1694) or Göttingen (1737), but others, such as Vienna in the last quarter of the 18th century, were inspired to emulate them. In general, the universities dominated intellectual and cultural life. Rulers valued them, and their teachers were influential, because they served the state by educating those who would serve. Leading academic figures held posts, enabling them to advise the government: the political economist Joseph von Sonnenfels was an adviser to the Habsburgs on the serf question. Lutheranism was another important factor in the evolution of the attitude to authority that makes the German Enlightenment so markedly different from the French. In the 18th century it was further influenced by Pietism, which was essentially a devotional movement though imbued with a reforming spirit. Nor was the earnest religious spirit confined to the Protestant confessions. In Maria Theresa's Austria, Jansenism, which penetrated Viennese circles from Austrian Flanders, was as important in influencing reforms in church and education as it was in sharpening disputes with the papacy. But there was nothing comparable, even in the Catholic south and Rhineland, to the revolt of western intellectuals against traditional dogma. Amid all his speculations, Leibniz, who more than any other influenced German thought, had held to the idea of a personal God not subject to the limitations of a material universe. It was devotion, not indifference, that made him, with Bossuet, seek ground for Christian reunion.

Leibniz's disciple, Christian Wolff, a leading figure of the Aufklärung, was opposed to the Pietists, who secured his expulsion from Halle in 1723. Yet, though he believed that reason and revelation could be reconciled, he shared with the Pietists fundamental Christian tenets. In Halle there emerged a synthesis of Wolffism and Pietism, a scientific theology that was progressive but orthodox. Pervading all was respect for the ruler, reflecting the acceptance of the *cuius regio, eius religio* principle; it reduced the scope for internal conflicts, which elsewhere bred doubts about authority. In translating conservative attitudes into political doctrines, the contribution of the lawyers and the nature of the law they taught were crucial. In place of the moral vacuum in which the single reality was the power of the individual ruler, there had come into being a body of law, articulated preeminently by Hugo Grotius in *On the Law of War and Peace*. It was grounded not only in proven principles of private law but also in the Christian spirit, though it was strengthened by Grotius's separation of natural law from its religious aspects. As expounded by Wolff and the historiographer Samuel Pufendorf, natural law endorsed absolutism. They did not wholly neglect civil rights, they advocated religious toleration, and they opposed torture, but, living in a world far removed from that of Locke or Montesquieu, they saw no need to stipulate constitutional safeguards. Wolff declared that "he who exercises the civil power has the right to establish everything that appears to him to serve the public good." Such a sovereign, comprising legislative, executive, and judicial functions, was also, as defined in Wolff's *Rational Thoughts on the Social Life of Mankind* (1756), a positive force, benevolent: he was Luther's "godly prince" in 18th-century dress, serving his people's needs. *Cameralwissenschaft* — the science and practice of administration — would serve the ruler by increasing the revenue and also improve the lot of the people.

Envisaging progress under the sovereign who created the schools, hospitals, and orphanages and provided officials to run them, Wolff was only one among numerous

writers who contributed to the ideal of benevolent bureaucratic absolutism, or *Wohlfahrstaat*. Though also influenced
by the local school of cameralists and 17th-century writers such as Philippe Wilhelm von Hörnigk and Johann
Joachim Becher, the emperor Joseph II, having the
largest area to rule and the most earnest commitment
to its principles, came to exemplify the Aufklärung. By
his time, however, there was a growing reaction against
the soulless rationality of the natural lawyers. With the
exception of the Prussian critic Johann Gottfried Herder,
whose ideal *Volk*-state would have a republican constitution, political thought was unaffected by the emphasis
of the literary giants of Romanticism on freedom and
spontaneity. His contemporary Kant, an anticameralist,
believed in a degree of popular participation but would
not allow even the theoretical right of revolution. In *Was
ist Aufklärung?* Kant drew a vital distinction between the
public and private use of one's reason. With the Prussian
king Frederick the Great in mind, he advanced the para-
dox that can be taken as a text for the Enlightenment
as well as for German history. The ruler with a well-
disciplined and large army could provide more liberty
than a republic:

> *A high degree of civil freedom seems advantageous to a people's
> intellectual freedom, yet also sets up insuperable barriers to it.
> Conversely, a lesser degree of civil freedom gives intellectual
> freedom enough room to expand to its fullest extent.*

THE ENLIGHTENMENT
THROUGHOUT EUROPE

Foreigners who came to see the monuments of Italy, or perhaps to listen to the music that they might recognize as the
inspiration of some of the best of their own, were likely to

return convinced that the country was backward. Its intellectual life might remain a closed book. As elsewhere, the Enlightenment consisted of small, isolated groups; measured by impact on governments, they had little obvious effect. Where there was important change, it was usually the work of a ruler, such as Leopold of Tuscany, or a minister, such as Bernardo Tanucci in Naples. The power of the church, symbolized by the listing of Galileo, a century after his condemnation, on the Index of Forbidden Books; the survival, particularly in the south, of an oppressive feudal power; and the restrictive power of the guilds were among the targets for liberals and humanitarians. Universities like Bologna, Padua, and Naples had preserved traditions of scholarship and still provided a stimulating base for such original thinkers as Giambattista Vico and Antonio Genovesi, a devout priest, professor of philosophy, and pioneer in ethical studies and economic theory. The distinctive feature of the Italian Enlightenment, however, as befitted the country that produced such scientists as Luigi Galvani and Alessandro Volta, was its practical tendency—as if speculation were a luxury amid so much disorder and poverty. Its proponents introduced to political philosophy utilitarianism's slogan "the greatest happiness of the greatest number." They also felt the passion of patriots seeking to rouse their countrymen. The greatest representative of the Italian Enlightenment was Cesare Beccaria, whose work included *Of Crimes and Punishments* (1764); in his lifetime it was translated into 22 languages. His pupils and imitators included Catherine II of Russia and Jeremy Bentham, the most influential figure in the long-delayed reform of English law. "Newtoncino," as Beccaria was called by admirers, claimed to apply the geometric spirit to the study of criminal law. There was indeed no mystique about his idea of justice. "That bond which is necessary to keep the interest of individuals united, without which men would return to their original state of barbarity," may recall the pessimism of Thomas Hobbes, but his formula for penalties answered to the enlightened ruler's search for what was both rational and practical: "Punishments which exceed the necessity of preserving this bond are in their nature unjust." So Beccaria condemned torture and capital punishment, questioned the treatment of sins as crimes, and stressed the value of equality before the law and of prevention having priority over punishment. Much of the best enlightened thought comes together in Beccaria's work, in which the link between philosophy and reform is clearly evident.

The Enlightenment was a European phenomenon: examples of enlightened thought and writing can be found in every country. There were important reforms in late 18th-century Spain under the benevolent rule of Charles III. There was little originality, however, about the Spanish Enlightenment, or *Luces*, and its disciples. The spirit of acceptance was stronger than that of inquiry; Spain apparently was a casebook example of the philosophes' belief that religion stifled freedom of thought. It was a priest, Benito Feijóo y Montenegro, who did as much as any man to prepare for the Spanish Enlightenment, preaching the criterion of social utility in a society still obsessed with honour and display. Conservatism was, however, well entrenched, whether expressed in the pedantic procedures of the Inquisition or in the crude mob destroying the marqués de Squillace's new street lamps in Madrid in 1766. "It is an old habit in Spain," wrote the conde de Campomanes, "to condemn everything that is new."

So the accent in Spain was utilitarian—more *Colbertiste* than *philosophe*—as in other countries where local circumstances and needs dictated certain courses of action. Johann Struensee's liberal reforms in Denmark (1771–72) represented, besides his own eccentricity, justifiable resentment at an oppressive Pietist regime. The constitutional changes that followed the first partition of Poland in 1772 were dictated as much by the need to survive as by the imaginative idealism of King Stanisław. Despite her interest in abstract ideals, reforms in law and government in Catherine the Great's vast Russian lands represented the overriding imperative, the security of the state. In Portugal, Pombal, the rebuilder of post-earthquake Lisbon, was motivated chiefly by the need to restore vitality to a country with a pioneering maritime past. Leopold of Tuscany was able to draw on a rich humanist tradition and civic pride. Everywhere the preferences of the ruler had an idiosyncratic effect, as in the Margrave Charles Frederick of Baden's unsuccessful attempt in 1770 to introduce a land tax (the *impôt unique* advocated by the physiocrats), or in Pombal's campaign to expel the Jesuits (copied supinely by other Catholic rulers).

Overall it may seem as easy to define the Enlightenment by what it opposed as by what it advocated. Along with some superficiality in thought and cynical expediency in action, this is the basis for conservative criticism: When reason is little more than common sense and utilitarianism so infects attitudes that progress can be measured only by material standards, then Edmund Burke's lament about the age of "sophisters, economists, and calculators" is held to be justified. Some historians have followed Burke in ascribing not only Jacobin authoritarianism but even 20th-century totalitarianism to tendencies within the Enlightenment. Indeed, it may be that the movement that helped to free man from the past and its "self-incurred tutelage" (Kant) failed to prevent the development of new systems and techniques of tyranny. This intellectual odyssey, following Lord Shaftesbury's "mighty light which spreads itself over the world," should, however, be seen to be related to the growth of the state, the advance of science, and the subsequent development of an industrial society. For their ill effects, the Enlightenment cannot be held to be mainly responsible. Rather it should be viewed as an integral part of a broader historical process. In this light it is easier to appraise the achievements that are its singular glory. To be challenged to think harder, with greater chance of discovering truth; to be able to write, speak, and worship freely; and to experience equality under the law and relatively humane treatment if one offended against it was to be able to live a fuller life.

CONCLUSION

Succeeding the Middle Ages, the early modern period of European history stretched roughly from the early 16th century, when it overlapped with the Renaissance, to the economic and political revolutions of the late 18th century. The opening decades of the early modern age brought economic expansion and social transformation. Early capitalism and protoindustrialization accompanied the growth of banking, finance, and trade, as well as the trans-Atlantic voyages that led to the exploitation of the resources of the New World and the beginnings of mercantilism. At the same time, tighter forms of social organization emerged, and communities were pressured by religious leaders to uphold uniform Christian beliefs. The emphasis on religious conformity fueled widespread witch hunts and the persecution of religious dissenters.

The early modern period also witnessed a newly adapted type of monarchy, based on the strong individual leaders of the new nation-states that were created at the breakup of the medieval order. Compared to their predecessors, the monarchs of this era were better able to monitor and manage their own societies, to exact more taxes, and to build mass armies that facilitated war and conquest. Early modern monarchs, such as the Holy Roman emperor Charles V, the French king Francis I, and the English queen Elizabeth I, unified their realms and strengthened their government bureaucracies.

Meanwhile, the religious revolution known as the Reformation gripped 16th-century Europe. Led by Martin Luther and John Calvin, the Reformation became the basis for the founding of Protestantism, one of the three major branches of Christianity. Having far-reaching political, economic, and social effects, it triggered the Roman Catholic Church's Counter-Reformation and protracted conflicts in the 16th and 17th centuries, including the Thirty Years' War.

Lasting from 1618 to 1648, the Thirty Years' War was essentially a struggle between the Holy Roman Empire, which was Roman Catholic, and a network of German towns and principalities that had embraced Protestantism. Fueled by the political ambitions of the various European powers, the conflict ultimately embroiled most of Europe. At war's end, the balance of power on the Continent had been radically altered, and the essential structure of modern Europe as a community of sovereign states had been established.

In the 17th and 18th centuries the traditional division of society into three main classes—nobility, clergy, and commoners—was complicated by the growing wealth and prominence of the bourgeoisie. The rise of the bourgeoisie, urban dwellers who worked for a living and invested money in property and business ventures, contributed to the growth of cities, which were centres of trade, banking, and manufacturing. As these urban activities became increasingly important, the basis of the economy began to shift away from domestic production.

During this time the absolutist form of monarchy prevailed in much of Europe. With the political power of both the church and local lords curtailed, early modern monarchs could pronounce the absolute authority of the nation-state. Consequently, monarchs, as heads of state, were able to claim their own unlimited authority. Louis XIV of France and Frederick II of Prussia were two of the European monarchs that epitomized absolutist rule.

By the 18th century the Enlightenment, a revolutionary intellectual movement that celebrated the use of reason, had gained wide assent. This new worldview instigated groundbreaking developments in literature, philosophy, and politics. Traditional religious studies were eclipsed by the individual thinker's pursuit of knowledge, freedom, and happiness. Perhaps most significantly, as the notion of individual rights gained prominence, the concept of a monarch's divine right to rule was eroded. The Enlightenment thus contributed to the outbreak in 1789 of a popular revolution in France that ultimately swept away the French monarchy. The French Revolution, along with the concurrent economic transformations that marked the beginning of the Industrial Revolution, launched the modern era of European history.

GLOSSARY

absolutist Government led by an all-powerful ruler.

alchemy A theoretical system that involved the effort to change lead into gold.

animist A belief that objects and natural phenomena such as thunder have conscious life.

bourgeois Related to the social middle class, capitalistic.

catholic "universal" Related to the idea of a universal church.

cumbrous Something that is heavy, clumsy, or awkward.

defenestration Tossing someone or something out of a window, or forcing someone from a political position or office.

empiricism The theory that everything that is known comes from experience, not theory.

enclosure The division of communal farmland into individually owned and managed plots.

Enlightenment A 17th- and 18th-century philosophical movement that emphasized the use of reason over accepted doctrines and traditions.

feudalism A political and economic system in medieval Europe based on the power of landholders over their tenants, who worked the land on which they lived to benefit the landowner.

fin de siècle The end of a century.

ghetto An area of a city where Jews were compelled to live.

Junker A German landowning aristocrat.

lettre de cachet A letter with an official seal allowing an individual to be imprisoned without trial.

Marrano A Jew in early modern Spain who officially converted to Christianity to avoid persecution; many still lived as Jews while professing Christian views.

mercurial Changeable.

nominalism The theory that there are no universal words and that, therefore, the fact that many objects can be described as, say, blue, does not mean that the general principle of blueness actually exists.

nucleated settlements Towns or villages that are organized and concentrated around a central point, rather than being spread out.

oligarchic Government controlled by a small group.

philosophe One of the writers and thinkers of 18th-century France who believed in the principles of the Enlightenment, such as the power of human reason.

preferment An office or position that was prestigious, profitable, or both.

primogeniture The eldest son's right to inherit all the property of his parents.

putting-out system A method of production in which a merchant purchased raw materials and distributed them to labourers for processing, usually in the labourers' homes. The merchant compensated the labourers for their work and then sold the finished products for his own profit.

quixotic Foolishly impractical, unpredictable.

Reformation Beginning in the 16th century, a religious movement marked by the rejection of Roman Catholicism and the establishment of Protestantism.

schism A formal division within a religious organization.

scrofula A tubercular condition, particularly of the lymph glands.

seigneur In France, the lord of a manor during feudal times.

transhumance The seasonal movement of livestock (such as cattle) between winter and spring pastures.

tyrannicide The act of murdering a despotic leader.

vassal An individual who serves a feudal lord.

worsted A type of cloth woven from yarn spun from long-haired wool that was lighter and cheaper to make than woolens.

yeomanry A class of small landowning farmers.

BIBLIOGRAPHY

The economic background of early modern Europe is discussed in E.E. Rich and C.H. Wilson (eds.), *The Economy of Expanding Europe in the Sixteenth and Seventeenth Centuries* (1967); and Jan De Vries, *European Urbanization, 1500–1800* (1984), a broader survey. Commerce and trade and their significance as characteristics of the home countries are treated in Ralph Davis, *The Rise of the Atlantic Economies* (1973). Early modern society is examined in Roger Chartier (ed.), *Passions of the Renaissance* (1989; originally published in French, 1986), a volume of essays dealing with the period from the Renaissance to the Enlightenment, from the series *A History of Private Life*. Brian Pullan, *The Jews of Europe and the Inquisition of Venice, 1550–1670* (1983), is an often poignant examination of ethnic relations.

Early modern politics and diplomacy are dealt with in many general histories of the 16th and 17th centuries. G.R. Elton (ed.), *The Reformation, 1520–1559*, 2nd ed. (1990); R.B. Wernham (ed.), *The Counter-Reformation and Price Revolution, 1559–1610* (1968); and J.P. Cooper (ed.), *The Decline of Spain and the Thirty Years' War, 1609–48/59* (1970), three volumes in *The New Cambridge Modern History* series, offer a sequence of chapters by various authors, thematically organized. H.G. Koenigsberger, George L. Mosse, and G.Q. Bowler, *Europe in the Sixteenth Century*, 2nd ed. (1989), treats the earlier part of the period. The last 50 years of the period, dominated by the genesis and course of Continental war, are best approached through Geoffrey Parker (ed.), *The Thirty Years' War*, rev. ed. (1987). Specific topics related to the Reformation and Counter-Reformation are discussed in Barbara Diefendorf, *Beneath the Cross: Catholics and*

Huguenots in Sixteenth-Century Paris (1991); and Mack Holt, *The French Wars of Religion* (1993). General surveys of the 17th and 18th centuries include Geoffrey Treasure, *The Making of Modern Europe, 1648–1780* (1985); M.S. Anderson, *Europe in the Eighteenth Century, 1713–1783*, 3rd ed. (1987); and William Doyle, *The Old European Order, 1660–1800* (1978, reprinted 1984). Specific social and demographic questions are explored in Michael W. Flinn, *The European Demographic System, 1500–1820* (1981); Pierre Goubert, *The French Peasantry in the Seventeenth Century* (1986; originally published in French, 1982); Jerome Blum, *Lord and Peasant in Russia: From the Ninth to the Nineteenth Century* (1961, reprinted 1971); and Guy Chaussinand-Nogaret, *The French Nobility in the Eighteenth Century: From Feudalism to Enlightenment* (1985; originally published in French, 1976).

The age of absolute monarchy is covered in J.H. Shennan, *The Origins of the Modern European State, 1450–1725* (1974); A.R. Myers, *Parliaments and Estates in Europe to 1789* (1975); Ragnhild Hatton (ed.), *Louis XIV and Absolutism* (1976); Derek McKay and H.M. Scott, *The Rise of the Great Powers, 1648–1815* (1983); and Jeremy Black, *European Warfare, 1660–1815* (1994). The interaction of thinkers and "enlightened" absolutism is explored in H.M. Scott (ed.), *Enlightened Absolutism: Reform and Reformers in Later Eighteenth-Century Europe* (1990).

The Enlightenment has attracted a vast literature, including Peter Gay, *The Enlightenment, an Interpretation*, 2 vol. (1966–69, reprinted 1977); Alan Charles Kors and Paul J. Korshin (eds.), *Anticipations of the Enlightenment in England, France, and Germany* (1987); Roy Porter and Mikuláš Teich (eds.), *The Enlightenment in National Context* (1981); S.C. Brown (ed.), *Philosophers of the Enlightenment* (1979); and Dena Goodman, *The Republic of Letters* (1994).

INDEX